ENDO

"I highly recommend this book for its profound wisdom to any leader of leaders; such is my dear friend Dr. Emmanuel Ziga."

Matthew Crouch
President–Trinity Broadcasting Network

"This man, a modern-day prophet, has a tried and true message. He has practiced this message. Now, the impartation of the messenger and the message will impact your life beyond description and expectation. The personal impact Emanuel Ziga has had on Jeannie and I would take a book to express. Several of my friends and influential leaders, of whom I work closely with, would say the same. Get ready for a life-changing experience."

Phil Munsey
Chairman, Champions Network of Churches with
Joel Osteen, Lakewood Church

"I recommend this book on leadership, The Power of One. Emmanuel Ziga is greatly used by God in Latin America. His words have edified pastors and leaders in our nation and continent. I am certain The Power of One will contribute to the growth of your personal leadership skills for the Kingdom of God."

Odilon Vergara
Senior Global Pastor Shalon Church – Curitiba, Brazil

"The teachings in this book will release many of God's hidden treasures that will accelerate your quest to achieve your purpose and destiny."

Bob Harrison
"Dr. Increase" – Harrison International

"The Power of One, by Emmanuel Ziga amazingly blends the depths of scientific study with newness of topic. This book is a blessing and an admonishment to even the most sophisticated minds."

Bishop Alexey Rudenky
Federation of Russian Churches – Volgograd, Russia

"The Power of One is a book of daring to believe! Emmanuel Ziga has the heart to see the generation of hidden 'Gideons' come to their place of responsibility and understanding of purpose in business, ministry and society at large. This book is an amazing faith building tool for us to see the breakthroughs needed in today's world."

Joseph Ewen
Leader of the River Network of Churches in Northeast Scotland
Board member of Antioch Ministries Intl.

"The Power of One teaches a very simple lesson - by tapping into the power inside of you and responding to the voice of God – you can add something to this planet that no one else can."

Neil Cameron
Senior Pastor of Apex Church
Superintendent of the Assemblies of God in Scotland

"Dr. Ziga has a deep and practical understanding of the enduring truths of scripture and how they apply in today's world. Enjoy this book and apply its timeless wisdom!"

Paul Szkiler
Author-"A Call To Business" Founder and CEO of
Truestone Impact Investment Mgt. – London, UK

"An entire generation of unknown leaders, across many spheres of social influence, have been waiting for this book. The Power of One, by Dr. Emmanuel Ziga has the potential to release a new phase of leaders who are currently in hiding while contending with a sense of personal inadequacy and deficiency. "

Dr. Wayne Malcolm Bishop,
London, UK

THE POWER OF ONE©

Your Singular Journey of Purpose,
Destiny & Leadership

DR. EMMANUEL ZIGA

emerge
publishing
TULSA, OKLAHOMA

24 23 22 21 20 19 18   1 2 3 4 5 6 7 8

THE POWER OF ONE — Your Singular Journey of Purpose, Destiny & Leadership
©2018 Dr. Emmanuel Ziga

Published by:
Emerge Publishing, LLC

TULSA, OKLAHOMA

9521B Riverside Parkway, Suite 243
Tulsa, Oklahoma 74137
Phone: 888.407.4447
www.EmergePublishing.com

BISAC Category:
REL012070   RELIGION / Christian Life / Personal Growth
REL012090   RELIGION / Christian Life / Professional Growth
SEL027000   SELF-HELP / Personal Growth / Success

ISBN: 978-1-943127-63-4 Paperback
ISBN: 978-1-943127-64-1 Digital

Printed in United States.

CONTENTS

ACKNOWLEDGMENTS

The impact of the Word of God has played a dominant role in shaping my life through the years. I am eternally grateful to the Lord Jesus who saved me, gave me eternal life, and His Holy Spirit to help me fulfill my mandate on the Earth. However, since no man is an island on the Earth, our success stories are always inter-woven with the influences of others and their achievements. I am humbled and grateful.

PREFACE

This book is designed to responsively provoke your thoughts about why you are here as an individual functioning in a distinct leadership office in such a time as this. It has in itself the different facets of the importance of your person who finds themselves in life's scenarios not created by yourself.

- If you have ever sat down to ask yourself, why am I here, and how come I get to do this? Then this book has your answers.

- If you have ever believed in your relevance and are confident in your abilities to help your generation, even more so, is this book for you.

- If you have never believed in your abilities, and yet have always been pushed forward into leadership by others, whose confidence in you to achieve more than you thought you could, then you need to read this book from cover to cover, more than three times.

- If you are just beginning your leadership journey, or find yourself at the end of your roles, the inspirations of this book are exactly what you may need.

• The considerations of this leadership literature I believe are indisputable thoughts for every mentor to use for discussions, instructions, and encouragements to your clients and students.
• There are values in this book that every political leader of the highest authorities should feed on.
• The young millennial, young professionals, and their networks, need the subjects discussed in this book at the forefront of their deliberations and meditations.

May your life's journey of leadership and its aspirations be full of great adventures, creativity, witty inventions and thought inspiring moments.

I dare the end results of your input into this world you came to meet, become an endless legacy to the generations you will never see or meet.

INTRODUCTION

The subject of social greatness, success, prosperity, influence, productivity, creativity, transformation, elevation, promotion, and more has always began with one man, one person, based on the principle of one. One can be defined as: alone, only, precise, particular, singular, sole, unique, uncommon, different, and definite. The power of one is one of God's hidden treasures revealed. The power of one has never failed; it has always produced results, but with its misunderstandings have also come failures and deceptions. I pray a fresh inspiration upon your life as you read this book: The Power of One, as in the glory of one, the inspiration of one, and the key of one.

The word "network" has become a usual thinking process in

the middle income to the upper echelon of successful communities. The inspiration to be successful has always bred the desire to drive a team or a social group of people to one goal, that is to network. Explained phonetically as "a net that works", a network is the aim for every above-average thinker to be part of a successful synergy of ascending individuals in life.

However, the genesis of every known network in history so far, has always begun from the thought of a man. The power of one is the womb of every network but the spine of every network needs the brain of a selfless individual, with a motivation to overtake the failure syndrome of a society, an industry, a community, or even a school. Networks always began from one thinking brain, in most cases an eternally chosen vessel of grace.

History has also proven the hijacking of a, Type A personality born to be great and a blessing, but can be turned around by evil forces to use their God given capacity to the disgrace of human excellence. It is my prayer that no vessel of potential power will ever again be hijacked and deterred away from the pathway of light, glory and positive fruitfulness in any time-frame. Help us O Lord and protect our time with the covering of your glory, grace, and mercy and inspiration; let that which is wrong always be defused in our hearts and let that which is right always be empowered in our hearts! Amen.

CHAPTER 1:

THE PRINCIPLE

Principle is the method of formation, operation or procedure exhibited in a given case. Being also defined as an accepted rule of action or conduct, it has always been the underscoring factor of God's Word, will and ways. The subject of this book, *The Power of One*, emanates from the principled nature and attribute of the Triune God yet functioning as one authority in all ways.

> *For there are three that bear record in heaven, the Father, the Word (Christ), and the Holy Ghost: and these three are ONE.*   **I John 5:7**

Certainly this scripture ascertains the awesome glorious functionality of three distinct personalities of the Godhead. Their ability to present themselves as one personality reveals their capacity, capability and authority in operation. This is an incredible revelation to behold. Being both the creators and holders of eternity and time, the Godhead operates and administers their counsel and purpose in the most succinct and flawless manner of accurate judgment in manifestation. Declaring things which are not yet fulfilled or done, from ancient times we see the effective establishment of divine pleasure and purpose in whatever they put their thoughts and foreknowledge into.

Having the records of the past, present and future, God effectively made both heaven and earth to prosper with the same principles, that is to say, that which makes heaven effective is designed to make the earth prosperous. The amazing ability of the Godhead operating as one, is the reason why He is able to choose one person in time, to manifest in fulfillment, what is decided. For every person that He calls there has always been a God-reason with foreknowledge. Having said that, the original intent of the record-holding God, is the reason why people are called in certain manners, in certain times and for certain assignments. This is all recorded throughout the history of mankind. This principle has not failed.

> *Remember the former things of old: for I am God,*
> *and there is none else; I am God, and there is none*
> *like me, declaring the end from the beginning, and*

from ancient times the things that are not yet done,
saying, My counsel shall stand, and I will do all my
pleasure: Calling a ravenous bird from the east, the
man that executeth my counsel from a far country:
yea, I have spoken it, I will also bring it to pass; I
have purposed it, I will also do it. **Isaiah 46:9-11**

The *one* God created Adam as *one*, called Noah as *one*, raised Abraham as *one*, Isaac and Jacob as individuals, and Moses as one. In Exodus 3:6 God introduced Himself to Moses as the God of Abraham, Isaac and Jacob pronouncing His eternal ability and design. He handled three different individuals in three different dispensations, separately and yet continuing the sequence of the same vision without flaw. Abraham, Isaac and Jacob were three separate human entities, yet functioning in the proclamation of one divine purpose, achieving the ultimate goal individually yet corporately. Moses being introduced to God perceives that it is God's time for him to be that *one* individual person with a specific, eternal assignment to be fulfilled. In Romans 8:29-30, Paul's letter to Rome by the inspiration of God indicates a process of the eternal records in God's thoughts about individuals He works with. In the natural time-frames, the God who foreknows every individual, is also He who:

1. Predestines
2. Calls
3. Justifies
4. Glorifies

This principle has measured and authenticated the true mandate of the works of the Lord through any person or people He lays His hands on. The God of records works in the most organized, predetermined plan of action for a desired goal towards glorification. The foreknowledge of God is the conclusive record dynamics of what is packaged, planned and designed in a lively state of being, in the thought of the Holy Trinity. The implementation of their thoughts establish an administered end of expectation to be revealed. The foreknowledge and predestined status of a person in God's mind to be established before the call, is an incredible and unfailing principle of the highest order. The sovereign leaders, being the Father, the Word (Christ) and the Holy Ghost in their leadership state of creativity, knowledge and excellence, see the end from the beginning. They set the path of successful mandates in place before releasing the chosen human vessel designed to carry it through, into the required mandate or calling. That is to say, the records of heaven must tally with expected works of every chosen man on earth.

> *After this, Jesus knowing that all things were now accomplished, that the scripture might be fulfilled, saith, I thirst.* **John 19:28**

By this scripture Jesus had to make sure that His deeds in the earth were in perfect accordance with what was written concerning Him before coming to the earth. So is the expectation of every chosen vessel of the Lord in time.

Then said I, Lo, I come: in the volume of the book it is written of me, I delight to do thy will, O my God: yea, thy law is within my heart. **Psalm 40:7-8**

Knowing however the weakness of men, heaven protects their mandate through the principle of justification. In other words overruling the probability of human weaknesses attempting stop the will of God, by the divine gifts, anointing, inspirations, visitations, impartation and directions as required. These are endowed on a person, to make him succeed no matter what, except by his own choice to fail. With the ultimate, wonderful plan of glory, we are called to bring much honor to God, the original record creator and master planner. For this cause we get to enjoy rewards through our obedience in walking the journey that was determined for our benefit and fulfillment. The influence of one personality becoming an authority in the manifestation of an ultimate purpose is first found in the character and nature of God. It is considered as one of the cardinal mysteries of the values of the Most High God in the operation, administration and manifestation of His will without fail.

Deuteronomy 6:4 states that, "Hear ye oh Israel, for the Lord thy God, He is one God. With reference to verse 3, which states the validity of the promise of a land of milk and honey. In His sovereignty this *ONE* God can handle the responsibility of bringing a people from the place of depravity, slavery, rejection and failure to an utmost success story; situated in a land most precious above all lands. The credibility of an amazing God revealed in the Holy Scriptures to work as one without fail, gives credence to why He is able to choose one person for an unbelievable vision-package which is literally impossible for an ordinary human being to fulfill. If God as *ONE* can create eternity and time with such perfection, then He can create *one* man on the earth to manage it. This is God Most High at work. He truly understands how to design human beings in His image and after His likeness, to the intent that they might function individualistically to achieve a glorious goal in a pluralistic environment.

Ephesians 4:1-15 says there is:

- One body
- One Spirit
- One calling
- One hope of your calling
- One Lord
- One faith
- One baptism
- One God
- One Father of all who is above all,
  through all and in you all.

To every one person that is called, is given heaven's grace for fulfillment. Jesus held captivity captive. He gave gifts of ministry to men; to some apostles, to some prophets, to some evangelists, to some pastors, to some teachers, for the perfecting of the saints, for the work of the ministry, for the edification of the body of Christ. (Ephesians 4:11-12). This incredible insight reveals the Kingdom network made up of individual persons loaded with God values, visions, gifts and offices. A formidable network of the "God-kind of people" set apart as a united force, gives strength and stature to His Kingdom, in the unity of Christ. I would say there has been a lot of discussion about networking, but understanding that the principle and strength of a network is found in its weakest individual, is essential. This amplifies the importance of one person in God's sight. If every individual can be successful in fulfilling God's plan, then we achieve the success story of a Kingdom where solid individuals create a bond of fellowship in a generation.

Apostles, prophets, evangelists, pastors, teachers, and all other gifts of ministry work together. They have their own anointing and offices which are designed to depend on each other, so as to strengthen our worship to God as one team in one Kingdom. Each office walks in the understanding of purpose interdependently yet individualistically. What perfect team work! A network of individuals creating the net worth of God's Kingdom. David's army was as formidable as the host of heaven, yet made up of individual warriors like Joash and Amasai, etc. (I Chronicles 12:1-13).

May you receive your revelation, catch your mantle like Elisha and move the Kingdom to the glory of God!

Every individual personality in the house of the Lord who understands their journey in destiny, is like a joint that supplies the beauty of the bigger picture, released from eternity into time. The Trinity of God reveals the Father, the Son and the Holy Ghost. They function effectively as *ONE* God with unfathomable excellence of greatness in power. This is the grace that thrives behind every individual person called of God to fulfill a divine agenda without fail. Romans 5:19 shows that by one man's disobedience, many were made sinners, so by the obedience of one, many have been made righteous. This incredible scripture ascertains the capacity of one man's influence through the generations when called of God.

Adam was the first man ever created in the image and the likeness of the ONE God in three Persons. The unbelievable capacity of influence he was given over the entire human race as *one man, is commendable and yet* highly underrated by himself. This is very unfortunate. Such presumptuous thinking processes seem to have plagued every human being that came after him. The power of self-underestimation is the mindset of assumption, for which cause Adam took the warning of God for granted and the fall of mankind ensued. The correction of this choice was through another *one Man,* as the second Adam, to restore the fallen nature back to the original state of glory, stature, image and likeness of God in righteousness.

In the Psalm 8:3-9, the Bible shows man who was set into a pedigree between the Holy Trinity and the angels of God. The incredible endowment of power was given to mankind for rule, management and dominion over all the works of God's hands. This scripture announces the amazement of someone who was shocked to see the incredible capacity entrusted to man. In other words, the same dominion potential in *one man* is in *all men*. Imagine the endowment of the God-kind of mandate to rule in one person. This explains why God sees the beauty of raising *an individual* to fulfill that which is required by his Creator. We are endowed with much skill, ability, capacity, capability and mandate to wonders.

> *May this faith be in you, knowing for a fact that there is nothing in the heavens, the earth or under the earth that is impossible for a man who is called of God for a divine purpose.*

He knows what He has put in you and therefore can place a demand on you to fulfill His will and pleasure at any given time. This is the reason why God is mindful of man, because of the splendid and creative intrigues He knows man has within. God is the best and He does the best, therefore He expects the best out of every one person, male or female.

Romans 9:23-24 refers to both gentiles and Jews appointed of God for His purpose as vessels of mercy. To the intent that we might all understand that the Almighty God's decision to use any individual is an act of mercy. Knowing very well that a perfect God is able to work intimately with imperfect beings to do the God-kind of works is nothing less than the devotion of grace and mercy. No one therefore should boast in himself but in the power of God that is able to make everyone succeed extraordinarily. If by one man's righteousness, vision can be restored to endless generations, then credence is given *to the principle of: The*

Power of One Man. This potentially brings untold blessings and direction to a generation that needs guidance.

In Acts 9:6-15 God zeroed in on Saul in the midst of a steaming human average with equal abilities for the job and yet He carved out of His grace, this individual vessel. Who would select a person like this brutal human destroyer of Tarsus? Ananias contested but God carried the day by not arguing and followed through with what was decided in eternity for that time. In other words, God demonstrated by action this one statement, *"I know what I'm about."*

The terminology, "a chosen vessel unto Me" states that God is proven to be a firm Creator-Leader whose stable plan of action justifies whoever is eyed by eternal glory, for a manifestation in time, demarcated for a unique assignment. At this point Saul's negative records didn't stop God nor mattered anymore but rather affirmed God's flawless principle of engagement to conclude what was started. Surely if God is FOR the chosen vessels of mercy who can be against them? Justified by faith and the cleansing power of the shared blood of Calvary, we all have hope to fulfill our course.

CHAPTER 2:

PRESERVATION

The definitive strength of one is the reason why preservation, as to protection, is important. Romans 9:29 says that if the Lord had not preserved for us a seed, we would have been as Sodom and Gomorrah, signifying that the preserved seed of one averted the corruption of endless generations; *the preservation of one.*

In politics and public governance, the president, the prime minister, the king, the queen, the chief executive, the personality at the highest helm of affairs is that *one seed* that should be protected, preserved and not exposed to unacceptable contentions because of the eternal principle of one that has never failed.

In science and technology, the inventions of many new things through the history of mankind have most often come out of one unknown person to all, but known to God; from Thomas Edison and Mark Zuckerberg to Bill Gates and so on. Who knows who this next one person could be?

May this book inspire the hidden greatness in you, May it stir up the embryo of a new stream of thinking that has been lying dormant in you! For what you know, you were raised for a time such as this.

The power of one could be the hinge of a door that determines how wide an opening the world can receive from your ideas into a new dimension of living, prosperity, liberty and solutions. A great life always begins from one seed thought. Preservation is simply a smart way to go; that one seed preserved is the value of endless tributaries of amazing wonders in generational advancement and eternal glories.

Preservation is defined as: to keep alive or in existence; also as to keep safe from harm or injury; to maintain and reserve or to spare. It is the reason why God protects with His glory, His name, His love and His angels because of how big, how powerful and how precious *one* is in His sight. If you were the only person on this earth, God would still have personally taken the responsibility for your protection and preservation from harm and injury. He is able to save the world a thousand times over again by the power of one seed; preservation therefore is key to every future. Please protect yourselves; submit yourself under

God's preservation and inspired covering.

Every seed is covered and protected by an outer layer. Chicken eggs are made up of three major segments. The innermost yoke is the embryo and covered by the albumen, which is the white fluid layer. The shell is the outer cover and thus stronger to protect the first two segments. The life is in the embryo. In all your investments it is wise to have a preservatory plan. Always have a backup to preserve your ideas, your thoughts, and your seed. As you load your computers with information, letters and documents, it is wise to have a copy so as to avert an accident of losing information. Hence one of the greatest investments in the field of technology is the development of security. In finance and economic planning there is always a need for a strong network of security principles for the system of economics to work effectively and stand the test of time In the human anatomy, with the incredible brainpower God made, He established memory as His preservatory key to store information for the growth and development of the human system, into what man was designed to be. It is believed that if the brainpower of man was turned into hydro energy, it could provide a supply of electricity to the entire city of Los Angeles, a city of manufacturing industries, entertainment, goods and services, etc. For this purpose, God encased the brain of a person in the skull with the seal of a subconscious mind. The human seed in the womb of a pregnant women also displays the powerful principle of preservation. The egg with the sperm develop together into a fetus, very well preserved and nourished in the placenta. This incredible master mind of preservation and protection is put in place as long as the baby is in the mother's womb; *the preservation of one.*

God in His most infinite wisdom and His most incredible glory, has established the value of one as His strategy for creation. If it works for God, it definitely works for us also. I therefore submit that the destruction of *one* is likely a potential destruction of the future of many generations. Consider this in your meditation all the days of your life. In sports and athletics, the victory of one man gives the whole nation the rejoicing of a gold metal. In American football, the touch down of one man, gives the entire team triumph over the opposing team. In the world of soccer, with a team of eleven players, the goal of one man gives the victory and the nations an opportunity to rejoice. A strong and well-protected team is defined by the degree of security and wholesomeness of every individual that makes up the team.

An impervious protection plan around a leader, a great visionary, and cardinal gift and a kingly seed, is synonymous to building a fire wall around a house or a community of great treasures. It is that same reason God sets angels around his people. It is the reason why great nations invest into national and international security as well as loyal international relations, particularly protecting the headship or leader. For instance the attempted assassination of United States President Ronald Reagan occurred on March 30, 1981, 69 days into his presidency.

While leaving a speaking engagement at the Washington Hilton Hotel in Washington, D.C., he and three others were shot by an assassin. President Reagan walked out a side door to the hotel -- a door used more than 100 times by presidents in the previous decade. Waiting roughly 15 feet away stood the assassin holding a .22-caliber revolver. The president waved to the crowd as he approached the open door of his armored limousine. In less than two seconds, the assassin fired off six shots. The presidential press secretary was hit. A Secret Service agent and a D.C. police officer were also wounded. One bullet hit the limousine's armored glass; another bounced off the car.

A lead security agent grabbed the president's shoulders and pushed him down into the limousine. At the same time another security agent shoved the president in the small of his back and slams the door shut. The motorcade bolted from the scene. Reagan was shot in the chest, just below the left underarm. He suffered a punctured lung and heavy internal bleeding, but prompt medical attention allowed him to recover quickly. Reagan lost more than 2½ quarts of blood. Doctors said he would have been within minutes of going into shock and dying, had they not been able to replace the lost blood so quickly after the shooting.

It is believed all of the normal Secret Service procedures were followed that day. However the assassin exploited a weak point in presidential protection. The fact that at the time, it was still easy to get close to the president at certain points was exploited. The analysis of one of the top presidential security team members said, "If we had been a split second slower, he could have been hit in the head."

(https://en.wikipedia.org/wiki/Attempted_assassination_of_Ronald_Reagan)

(http://www.cnn.com/2011/POLITICS/03/30/hinckley.presidential.protection/)

God gives us His favor to make a difference as a gift from heaven but it is within our human volition to attach vital importance to preserve and protect what we have, with strength and wisdom. Both life and leadership are gifts from the Lord with the purpose of making posterity a desired dream of fulfillment and contentment. The Apostle Paul said, if the Lord had not preserved for us a seed (Christ), we would have been as Sodom and Gomorrah. May we never second guess the importance of the preservation of one. It has worked in the time's past and will work forever. The grace of one shall preserve the value of the multitude.

A powerful social economic system of every nation should be designed for the preservation of every one singular citizen and person. The careless handling of one person in a nation is a reflection of the ineffectiveness of political governance. The protection, the preservation and the security of one life is the multiplication of the preservation of the nation as a whole. So it is for every family unit in the house, every house in a county or district, every county or district in a region, state or province, every region, state or province in a nation, and every nation or country in a continent and every continent on the global scene. Without the importance of the preservation of one, there can be no effective value of the entire human society. May the Spirit of eternal preservation come upon us in our time, in our generation. In conclusion, the preservation of one equals the protection of many. It begins with one. One becomes the stem; one becomes the spine; and one becomes the pillar which carries the glory. Therefore, let's protect the one. *Welcome to the incredible strategy of the power of one and its preservation to the prosperity of the majority.*

CHAPTER 3:

ONE MAN

God has done awesome things by the mystery of one man. The strength of one fallible person with the backing of an infallible God creates a synergy of unbelievable results for the benefit of multiple generations. This is to say, God does things in 'ones' to effect limitless changes. The cross of Christ, His crucifixion, death and resurrection happened one time. Everybody on this earth gets to live once. The day of Pentecost was one time. The 120 disciples in the upper room were ten times more than the original twelve lieutenants of help and mission (Acts 1:15). The number ten stands for responsibility and explains how the Pentecost experience was God's action package for kingdom generations. It was to transfer responsibility into the hands of chosen vessels anointed by the Holy Spirit for results.

A FLAMING TORCH

A leader is a singular person but leadership is a system created by a team of leaders. In Acts 3:3 cloven tongues of fire sat upon each of them proving that God, although sovereign, still has a distinct focus on the individual. On the day of Pentecost, in the upper room was a network of seasoned people with one mind, in one accord and in one place. God in His sovereignty gave each singular person the attention of a lifetime. The endowment of power for each person was revealed by the *cloven tongues of fire*. This endowment was the infilling of the Holy Ghost in a unique way. This act proved how God uniquely gives every individual person a flame for action as a team, yet distinguished by specific mandates, course of action and purpose. It takes the aggregate of individual purpose-driven governance to execute a network essential above the ordinary. The best football team is made of skillful individuals with a serving heart to make a difference. So does every singular person in God's Kingdom receive a flame to be unique in God's team. Distinguished by cloven tongues of fire, these 120 persons were subject to the momentum that changed the course of history. With the cloven tongues of fire came their unique role, understanding, distinctness, zeal, wisdom, and consecration to the vision, identity and clarity of purpose.

- Thomas who was in the upper room, eventually took the vision to India.
- James took command of the project in Jerusalem to greater heights.
- Peter shifted into a universal-thinking drive and structured the global initiative.
- John closed the entire Holy Scriptures with the incredible book of Revelation.
- No telling the impact of Matthew, the former IRS tax collector.
- Bartholomew and the rest of the numbers played their roles and took their stand as individuals driven by the firepower of God, consumed by the grace of our Lord.

For every individual poised to see the extension of God's handiwork, I think it will be very helpful for you to receive your personal package of cloven tongues of fire. It characterizes illumination and exemplary excellence if handled with respect, obedience and uprightness. It makes you stay the course, overcome yourself and every contrary subject matter.

Every visionary is a flaming torch from God with a unique grace that heals and directs as well as comforts and strengthens, all who connect to His purpose. You are a flaming torch of God's vision that gives others vision and God's dream, that gives others a dream to live and die for.

There is a true story of a man of God in the USA who went to speak at a conference as a visiting guest speaker. On a particular

Saturday morning, he took the time to wind down on a beautiful sunny day, wearing his khaki shorts, yet dressed decently, he went to the mall with his wife. They moved from shop to shop as the wife was window-shopping. Apparently in the same city, was a terminally sick lady in bed praying for God's help of healing. That Saturday morning, she felt the strong prompting of the Holy Spirit to go to the mall and stand at the main entrance at a particular time. While standing there in obedience, she happened to look into the mall and saw a flame of fire, in a man, who walked in and out of the shops, as if he was window shopping. Very enthused about this vision, which she saw, as it were a walking flame of fire, beaming like light, she walked zealously towards this person sensing the draw of the Holy Spirit.. When she got to the person, it was the man of God that had been speaking in the city at this huge conference. In her amazement, she screamed, "It is you, it is you man of God!" The man of God, not knowing the vision she was seeing said, "What do you mean it is me?" After she narrated the story, he placed his hand on her, prayed for her and she was healed instantly.

Every visionary is as a flaming torch from God with a unique grace that can be a solution to several needs. Fulfilling the mandate can also establish the healing and restoration of the weakened and lost dreams of others. This is why a true purpose-driven person who has found his calling and walks in it, becomes a symbol of strength, hope, illumination and for that matter, a comforting covering for many to be nurtured and grow into their purpose. You are as a flaming torch of God's vision for a generation whose manifestation is designed to create a platform for others to succeed.

> *For with thee is the fountain of life: in thy light shall*
> *we see light.*   **Psalm 36:9**

The scripture above, explains how the leadership that comes out of a thriving vision can multiply success stories to many generations. Vision is a fountain of life because it gives relevance and direction to everyone. It is also a light-producing tendency that activates illumination out of obscurity. No telling how many oppressed citizens of life discover their niche when they connect to a vibrant and a thriving success story. This creates a sphere of influence that becomes the threshold and staying power for all to succeed no matter what.

Successful stories become point of references.

Everybody wants to be successful and therefore needs to be successful. Just as the flaming torch of an Olympic opening ceremony that sets ablaze a huge basin of a flammable substance on contact, I pray that your potential would be ignited to open the gates for unprecedented celebration of great journeys of purpose, inspiration, destiny, and true leadership. Furthermore every person that is born into this world is potentially a flammable material, as in the Olympic torch bowl. However, it takes contact and connection to an existing flame to be ignited. It is essential for that matter for the right kind of flame and light to come your way.

For example on the Day of Pentecost, all 120 people in the upper room, were potential flames of God's fire, waiting to be ignited. It happened in Acts 2:3. With the cloven tongues of fire burning as a flame on each of them, the light of their purpose was turned on and that light activates flavor for a higher life. Fifteen chapters later they turned the world upside down (Acts 17:6). This is to say, the flame that God set in their lives, by the outpouring of the Holy Ghost, became the light that was drawing the attention for universal change. Hebrews 1:7 says that God made them as His ministers of the flames of fire. May this heavenly flame of God's intentions for our lives, create light for change and impact.

LIGHT PRODUCES SALT

The scripture says, you are the light of the world and the salt of the earth (Matthew 5:13-16). Light creates salt. This is proven because in the beginning God created light before salt was made. This is to say, since light is the source of all creativity, God being light Himself, makes salt the produce of light. Furthermore since metaphorically salt represents influence, we see how light influences all things that must have influence. This therefore sets the tone of the principle that all things come from light, because God is light.

We see for instance how public figures on the global scene and Hollywood celebrities influence the taste of fashion and morals that are emulated by many who focus on them, good or bad. Every positive light determines the availability of constructive taste which influences spiritual and socioeconomic emphasis and direction, to say the least. This is to say, if you can be the light, you can be the salt for double influence.

Having said that, as salt activates thirst, so your leadership stirs up the passion for many to change their course of direction for greater profit in life. Furthermore it also becomes a consistent agent of self-thirst for progressive thinking, creativity and excellence. It makes you always reach for personal higher goals and standards within yourself. It is not possible to impact the outside word effectively without first conquering your personal inner challenges and controversies. The salt in you is the provoker of hunger for higher heights. It contributes to making you a relevant sharp threshing instrument required to be on the cutting edge of every aspect of personal and group leadership. It maintains your inner self-value and staying power for successful living. It keeps your mind, will and emotions salted with the grace for exclusive and distinguished personal cultures. This is to say, leadership and its saltiness begins from the inside to impact the outside world effectively. I would dare to say therefore, that there is always one salted person or thought out there that ignites the glory of a changing demography. Salt activates paradigm shifts at all times! There can be no real direction without the influence of salt and its guiding abilities.

If someone says, "Lets make a change."
You should ask, "Who is the salt?"

The thirstier society becomes because of the flavor of

influence she tastes, the more energized she becomes for change in the right direction. This is how strategic your flame of purpose is designed to be. Let nothing quench your flame and may no-unforeseen circumstance cut you off before time. For instance King David, on his last appearance on the battle field, was cornered by an agile Philistine enemy, who had a new sword or a fresh strategy of war. Fatigued and weakened by age, David was rescued by his armor bearer, Abishai. The scare of Israel heightened with the thought that the king who was the light and the star of the nation, could have been cut off before his time. They said to the king,

> *"Thou shalt go no more out with us to battle, that thou quench not the light of Israel."*

> **(II Samuel 21:16-17)**

It is noteworthy to see how the next generation of soldiers protected David, their patriarch, from death by their vigilance over him. Therefore, it is recorded that David served his generation according to the will of God (Acts 13:36). May you go the long haul without fail and may the rising star that you are, be preserved to the end. It is important for us to keep a close eye on our leaders to secure the destiny of the future of the nation and their generations. Your generation needs your light and saltiness. Certainly it is prudent to keep a strong fire-wall around you, your destiny and purpose in God. Your light produces saltiness. Your saltiness produces influence. Your influence produces cycles of growth for many. May the impact of your light change the tasteless flavor of many, into a meaningful success story or contentment.

I believe once again the time has come for the emergence of sound-minded leaders to influence the influencers of the nations into the absolutes of distinction, excellence and creative breakthroughs.

The true story of Dr. Paul Crouch Sr. and his wife Jan is a relevant script of salt influencing generations. The conception of God's seed vision in their spirit and their ability to follow through with self-discipline, focus and hardcore obedience, gives credence to *the power of one* changing countless generations without end. Introducing Christian television in a generation that had never seen it before must have been quite a challenge. The simultaneous cycles of endless miracles, one feeding into the other, created waves they rode into breaking systematic records, positioning Trinity Broadcasting Network where it is today. With two satellites in orbit, coupled with several scripture-based programs globally, this is no doubt a parable of salt influencing endless generations, tribes, languages and cultures, extending from the north pole to the south pole of planet earth to date.

THE LEADERSHIP CHASSIS OF PURPOSE

The investment of God's incredible anointing in leaders is a notification and a landmark for one's lifetime journey into eternity. It is also a passageway of partnership with God as a chassis is to an engine. Whereas every building foundation is static in one place, the chassis of an automobile are not. They're made up of a set of frames, connected by a differential and suspension with four wheels. This mechanism carries the engine machinery or battery that drive the vehicle.

God made you and Him to work as a pair of chassis, which wheels the engine of purpose. This is to say, whereas God is one frame, He is connected to the frame of His leaders. The synergy of engagement carries the engine of destinies, so is the value of leaders in the hand of God. Every individual leader is the other chassis frame that moves generations to their place of glory. May the cloven tongues of Holy Spirit fire power, engage your indulgence for destiny, purpose and prosperity. With your life filled with the cloven tongues of fire, you become a leading system and a flaming torch in the hand of God, sent into the universe to implement what is required. Let the Lord serve you with His glorious light so you can serve the generation you have come to know with impact. You are a leading, flaming torch that sets others on their pathways with vision, clarity and results.

> *But the path of the just is as the shining light, that shines more and more unto the perfect day.*

Proverbs 4:18

As the anointing burns in you, your pathway gets brighter and brighter until the ultimate day of rewards. May you humbly serve eternity and time with the hand of God upon your life.

TIME AND SUCCESS

Time has proven that the longest lasting fruit of major prosperous breakthroughs have come out of one solitary life. The book of Judges in the Bible records an interesting story of Gideon the Judge, to this effect. In Judges 6:12-16 the Angel of the Lord visits a young lad whose family was the poorest in the tribe of Manasseh and of which Gideon was the least in his father's house. Needless to say that he was the most unlikely individual to become a shining light and a keynote deliverer of his people from insurmountable oppression, depression, frustration, and colossal captivity.

> *And the angel of the LORD appeared unto him, and said unto him, The LORD is with thee, thou mighty man of valor. And Gideon said unto him, Oh my Lord, if the LORD be with us, why then is all this befallen us? and where be all his miracles which our fathers told us of, saying, Did not the LORD bring us up from Egypt? but now the LORD hath forsaken us, and delivered us into the hands of the Midianites. And the LORD looked upon him, and said, Go in this thy might, and thou shalt save Israel from the hand of the Midianites: have not I sent thee? And he said unto him, Oh my Lord, wherewith shall I save Israel? behold, my family is poor in Manasseh, and I am the least in my father's house. And the LORD said unto him, Surely I will be with thee, and thou shalt*

smite the Midianites as one man. **Judges 6:12-16**

The true statement of God volunteering Himself to work with Gideon explains the partnership between God and man as the chassis of a vehicle operates. The power of one is designed to be extremely effective because the original intent of God to influence that one person, thought, or principle. In other words its ability to be explosively prosperous is hidden in the invisible partnership of God.

Many times the focus of one becomes the handicap around that singular mind. The invitation of God for one individual life to join His team of social transformation, is dependent on trust in God as well as God's confidence in man. There has never been a time when the strength of God was not made available to a willing vessel called of God. The partnership between God and man has always been the determination of heaven to answer the earth's questions, which have always existed with no surprise to God. As it is said, a thousand years is as one day to God, so also is one day able to change the destiny of a thousand years, with God using just one man. The power of one thought of wisdom dropped into the mind of one man from heaven creates ripples of a lifetime on the oceans of creation. The verbiage of the Angel of the Lord assigned to Gideon was very empowering to the young man. Imagine the overwhelming data of failure around the young man where he had to hide behind a wine press with such fear for which cause his people were paralyzed by the supremacy of enemy wickedness.

With the intention of Israel's enemies to annihilate their country, heaven comes on the scene and speaks a word to define the purpose of this one man Gideon, calling him a mighty man of valor. If God can bring valiance out of weakness, strength out of failure and success out of poverty, then there is not one in our generation that cannot be used by Him to change the course of history. There can be plenty in the midst of poverty and light in the midst of darkness. God searches to find that *one man* upon whom He can put the mantle of valiance, strength and the inspiration to overcome on; *it all begins from one man. The angel said, thou shall smite the Midianites as one man.* Heaven did not see any credibility in the weakness announced by Gideon. I therefore want to say, DO NOT give credibility to failure; DO NOT give your powerful words to the mystery of impossibility.

God consistently exemplifies success in every thing He does, focusing on the positive and the affirmative for with God nothing is impossible. Therefore working with God demands every one man to speak possibility, to walk possibility, trusting God to give the power of attorney to one single man, to tap into His grace and help in time of need because valiance is a gift of God; so also is victory and success. There are many who have worked hard and still do, but yet have not seen the success they desired over the years, but with one unction from God comes victory. The power of one man is an act of God upon the individual. The battle is not for the strong, neither victory for the mighty; the race is not for the swift, neither glory in the hands of the smart; but grace and mercy comes from the Lord upon the one He chooses to be His *one man*.

The true fact the chassis principle is also to say, that it carries the weight of the engine and the vehicle. I wish I could say, that your partnership with God eludes you from weights, the pressure and the stress it brings. Handling your own dream and vision can be very stressless because you have no standards to shoot for. You do everything at your own pace and you are of your own. As much as you can create pain, there are higher levels of challenges when you are in an inseparable partnership drive with God. He is so huge, so big and so glorious that following Him at His pace can create unsurmountable weights of difficulty, unless by the help of His Spirit. The synergy between you and Him can make the burden comparatively light, and its yoke easy. The Lord's will is his bill. I pray you stay connected and coherent as the chassis is made compact, strong and capable of functioning effectively. As the chassis keeps the entire machine of the vehicle together for one cause of the vision, so also we become totally inseparable and almost having the same DNA with our God in vision, passion, drive and goal setting. The chassis of purpose is a principle of effective interdependence with God and vice versa, to produce every one major breakthrough result. You are a *one-compact-machinery* in God's Spirit that influences generations without fail.

But he that is joined unto the Lord is one spirit

1 Corinthians 6:17-19 KJV

Partnership with men produces human results, but with God, your results are far above every human average. Be as a compact in God for the most glorious impact the world has ever known. You are the one to do this.

———————————

CHAPTER 4:

HANDICAP

The difficulty of man's ability to connect with God and to be what God wants him or her to be and do what God wants him or her to do, is usually limited by handicap. Gideon was fatally handicapped in his own mind. His handicap was based on:

- The prevailing circumstance of his nation, family and tribe.
- His own mindset, thought processes and beliefs about himself.
- His family status and pedigree.

These three factors are prevalent in every individual's life. We are all influenced by the environment, thoughts and family affairs. He was handicapped.

Handicap is defined as: any disadvantage that makes success more difficult. The natural inclination of every handicapped personality is to second-guess their abilities and capacities. "I am the least in the family" he said, "and where are all the miracles our fathers spoke about our God?" (Judges 6:15) I don't think any *logical thinker* should fault Gideon because of the influence of logic. Logic makes you think, see, and believe things horizontally; which is to say you just get used to what you say and you accept the logic of the circumstances. That's just what it is. The vertical analysis connects you to your belief in God vertically, but faith lifts you up and makes you float on the ocean of God's glory. Faith therefore makes you change your natural circumstance; it doubts your doubts and weakens your weaknesses as well dis-empowering your handicap. Faith does not negate the facts, but changes them. Hallelujah!

The predomination of the 'handicap syndrome' in the life of man creates controversies within that person, therefore how long will you continue to stand between two opinions within your own mind? How long will you continue to be torn apart between your spirit and your soul? In Judges 6:12, the voice of the angel carried the powerful prophetic word, "You mighty man of valor, you mighty man of valor." To imagine the weaknesses and negative beliefs of Gideon being knocked out by the Angel of the Lord who literally ignored all the arguments of a weak man. Heaven always overrules and interferes in the affairs of men. Thank God that He is our help in time of need. May God always overrule our weaknesses! May the Word of God concerning us take dominion over the deception we go through, because of fear, phobia and handicaps.

CHAPTER 5:

CONTROVERSIES

The uniqueness of every man determined to excel in his generation creates controversies; so is every trail blazing, cutting edge leader. As many as have *knowledge for witty inventions,* usually fall within the category of "controversial people" in society. Good is always controversial in the eyes of bad, as is light in the eyes of darkness. Influence therefore inspires people to do what they originally didn't think could be done, often times causing controversy. Controversy is one of the hallmarks of true success stories. A controversy is the coalition of two opposing opinions with each vying for control.

A controversy is defined as: contention, strife and argument; A prolonged public dispute concerning a matter of opinion; a debate. I have discovered through people's life stories that there is no success without controversies, often times including spoken and unspoken disputes in the eyes of the public. If a third party was to analyze God's choice of Gideon to be the one who restores the sovereignty, dignity and glory of his nation, one might ask, "Why would God choose a man like him? We know him. He is a failure and full of complexes; never stable minded. He has a poor self image, he can't be the chosen man for the job. Why would God not choose Gideon's father or maybe his uncle? Why from the tribe of Manasseh and not the tribe of Judah?"

Controversies happen when *the mind of the logical* loses gravity around the *illogical. It is even often said,* "It doesn't make sense!" May you never allow controversies to pull you down! May you never allow the controversies of the public to discourage you. The history of Jesus Christ proves Him to be an outstanding leader of all history. His time on this earth set new standards, new ways, and new dimensions of belief and connectivity with God far above the social grip of the Pharisaic, Saddusaic and Herodian religious doctrines, which were obviously contrary to the perfect will of God the Father.

In John 7:11-19 there is a clear incident of controversy surrounding Jesus Christ and His doctrine. The true fact of life is, that there is usually difficulty around change. Unfortunately, it is an average yet carnal tendency to resist change when it comes, whether good or bad. The average person has the tendency to settle for the usual and the common; it is considered as living a life of *common sense.* Everyone who follows the principles of *common sense* becomes common. This mindset diffuses the individual's uniqueness, which is often the key to the next developmental phase of a generation.

Jesus Christ, the Son of God, the Light of the world, was severely resisted because He came from a different order and a different approach, yet His life produced "off-the-chart results" that changed the world forever. The time-line of life is divided in two, because of Jesus, B.C. and A.D. A Messiah born in a manger, the King of kings as He is, but dies on the cross accepting the sin and faults He was innocent of. Though accepted as condemned and not truthful, He resurrected from the dead on the third day being accepted as truthful. Christ the Messiah, the Savior of the world, the wisdom of God and the joy of many generations gives everybody who believes in Him eternal fulfillment and abundant life.

In John 7:25-46 the populace are amazed at Christ's wisdom, eloquence, and brilliance. The amplified and outspoken controversial opinions of His truthfulness divided the society. Some questioned if He was the Christ, some said that He is the Christ, others believed He was a prophet, and expected Him to be born in Bethlehem of Judea.

> *So there was a division among the people because of Him; and some of them would have taken him; but no man laid hands on Him.* **John 7:43-44**

Police officers sent religious leaders to apprehend and arrest Jesus, but they couldn't because of the grace and strength, which came out of Him, to touch their lives. They said, "Never a man spake like this man." Such is the culture of trailblazers. The uniqueness with which God created every man makes every person ever born on earth, unique. In each human being there is a quality, a gift, a calling, a mandate, and a gene--which if allowed to be developed--by the grace of God, could be unusually spectacular yet still creating controversies. Therefore controversy can be a good thing because it is the hallmark of uniqueness.

May you excel, succeed, and rise up to be the standard bearer you were designed to be right in the hands of the Lord.

The power of one man has all it takes to be a shining light to a generation. May you never look down upon yourself nor judge your capacities based on the opinions and the influence of society. Avoid second guessing your abilities and meditate on the Word of God. It will deposit the wisdom and strength you need to be the blessing society is in need of.

> *And many other signs truly did Jesus in the presence*
> *of His disciples, which are not written in this book:*
> *But these are written, that ye might believe that Jesus*
> *is the Christ, the Son of God; and that believing ye*
> *might have life through His name.* **John 20:30-31**

The databank of God's records stirs up belief and possibility in everyone that desires to excel. For as much as God could use one young man, by the age of 33, to impact life and change the thought processes of the human race, past, present and future,

44

for all of eternity, so He also gives hope to anyone who believes. In the world of average-thinkers, the God of heaven can use you to do the impossible.

> *This is the disciple which testifieth of these things, and wrote these things: and we know that his testimony is true. And there are also many other things which Jesus did, the which, if they should be written every one, I suppose that even the world itself could not contain the books that should be written. Amen.*

John 21:24-25

I pray the same inspiration that empowered Jesus as one man to excel, exceed and produce Kingdom results in three years (that all the books in the world today cannot contain the volume of His activity) would also come upon you! As you flip through the pages of this book, may the love of God and grace of our Lord Jesus Christ and fellowship of the Holy Spirit overtake you with power and creative thinking to exceed your expectations as one man. The God who told Gideon that "thou shall smite the Midianites as one man" and made Jesus excel as one man, is about to make you an enigma of unspeakable breakthroughs which the world is yet to see!

God could have put gold and silver in the skies above us all but chose to place it into dirt and ground we walk across. If gold and silver are so precious, why do we walk over them before they're mined? Things we overlook become things held dear. God seems to endlessly advance His beauty on the stages of controversy; even the salvation of mankind which angels look into with untold amazement and awe.

> *Searching what, or what manner of time the Spirit of Christ which was in them did signify, when it testified beforehand the sufferings of Christ, and the glory that should follow... which things the angels desire to look into. Wherefore gird up the loins of your mind, be sober, and hope to the end for the grace that is to be brought unto you at the revelation of Jesus Christ.* **1 Peter 1:11-13**

The Messiah to be born in a manger is something no logical mind will think about, but God did this in spite the controversy and still made Him the King of Kings of kings and the Lord of lords. Great leaders are often controversial but they become influential after they have prevailed over adverse opinions. True impactful influence is the product of overcoming controversies and adversities.

Eyes haven't seen you yet, ears haven't heard you yet, the heart of man has not comprehended yet, the discovery that you are in our time. You are the one the world is about to celebrate! You are the one the world is about to congratulate. You are that one that is about to bring a smile on the face of this planet. *The power of one solitary life!*

CHAPTER 6:

GRACE

The dynamics of grace in the Old Testament differs from the New Covenant. The entire Bible, which is divided into law and grace, reveals the nature and sovereign magnanimity of God. The laws of Moses were very stringent because they came in the days when curse was a law; as pronounced on Adam and Eve in their disobedience. This scenario caused God to reveal favor to the recipients in very rare circumstances. Selected individuals and sometimes chosen groups of people enjoyed loving kindness other than grace. This gesture of the Most High was to keep His purpose alive and productive until the ultimate price paid on the cross. The Old Testament segment therefore caused God to allow fleecing and various extra proofs to help the faith of the badly damaged moral of the human race because of the curse. The law of Moses was a tough framework with stringent consequences,impossible to bear.

The story of Gideon records an angelic annunciation of his future and greatness. Without his personal invitation, God who had eternal plans for a man, who seemed to be failing in his day, brought new life, strength, productivity, and success. It made him overcome every limitation and suddenly brought him to a new standard of heights and glory. This is grace at work in the life of *one man* set to make history. Everybody needs grace on this earth. It is therefore God coming down to the level of the fallen human nature, so as to lift humanity to the utmost level of effectiveness, according to the original plan. This purpose of transformation into unbelievable standards of productivity, results and glory is what grace is all about. The unmerited favor of the God-kind is available to anyone who chooses to receive His plan for their lives. *The power of one* becomes the glory of many by the act of God's grace, which never fails.

The presence of grace is the announcement of victory over weakness; it is the foundation for limitless heights, setting new breakthrough records and grace standards. Every act of God's grace sends controversial ripples. Can a man do these things? Can he have these kinds of achievements? Yes, because grace empowers the weak to be strong and the blind to see. Grace negates the logic of controversy and establishes the handiwork of God through the vessels that are available and willing to be used by God.

The story of a weakened person, family, school, organization, business or generation, does not determine the outcome of the future. It is the release of the grace of God into circumstances, which were considered as condemned and hopeless, that determines the outcome. Grace turns our sorrows into dancing, our mourning into joy; giving us beauty for ashes. God's grace is great power to excel beyond human levels. Grace brings liberty from handicap. It is therefore refreshing and very needful; it is welcomed news to every man on this earth in whose nostrils there is breath. It is not a luxury but a necessity in order for success to be tangible, real, and worth celebrating.

The nature of God is revealed in three dimensions: His word, His will, and His ways. It is vividly depicted and clearly revealed through time that the Most High God has an unquenchable passion to handle the most difficult and impossible situations of creation. He loves to work with the weak things to confound the wisdom of the logical world and the base things to confound the high and the lofty. The appearance of the divine factor (the God phenomenon) is the arrival of supernatural empowerment called grace on the scene of impossibility. Where weaknesses abound, grace so much more abounds because God is a sovereign success thinking authority. His ways are far higher and so are His thoughts. The frequency of His activities, far outweigh our best abilities, which He knows and understands very well. The scripture says in Psalm 103:14 that He understands our frame and knows our weaknesses, this is why He sent His angel to Gideon. Consider that Gideon did not ask for a divine intervention, but rather God moved sovereignly into the situation and turned his story around.

I once visited a friend whose property bordered a flowing stream full of salmon. As we admired this clean water flow, surrounded with beautiful foliage, he suddenly directed my attention to look above the trees and said, "This great river has its source from that mountain, whose tip is far above the forest of trees before us." Sometimes God erects a solitude or singular person with the purpose of producing a source of life for many generations of families and much habitation to thrive and prosper effectively by. In perspective, imagine how much sustenance the stream is producing. Such is the beauty of God which begins as a river of life from one individual whose life has found its place in the hand of an active God of beauty, purpose, glory, and fruitfulness.

It takes a breath of life to find roots in a God driven by purpose and kindness to change the world. Moses said in Psalm 90:1, "Lord, thou hast been our dwelling place in all generations." Here Moses recounts the goodness of God and His sovereign glory released over the lives of those who offer themselves as available individuals. He appeals to God in his humility by asking Him to teach us to number our days that we may apply our hearts unto wisdom. It takes God to make one individual a power of joy to limitless generations. May the Lord beautify His great works in our lives.

So teach us to number our days, that we may apply our hearts unto wisdom. Return, O Lord, how long? and let it repent thee concerning thy servants. O satisfy us early with thy mercy; that we may rejoice and be glad all our days. Make us glad according to the days wherein thou hast afflicted us, and the years wherein we have seen evil. Let thy work appear unto thy servants, and thy glory unto their children. And let the beauty of the Lord our God be upon us: and establish thou the work of our hands upon us; yea, the work of our hands establish thou it.

Psalm 90:12-17

It takes a one-man principle to produce and sustain a productive network. It is noteworthy that every incredible network of like-minded people has come out of the thought of a single person. As the source of a river begins from a small geyser and springs into a huge river with fish and an entire aqua community, so is the generation of a network from a person. It is amazing to see the power of a great athlete of a nation and how great the joy they bring to a nation. The strength of a one vibrant man becomes the wisdom around which a social culture evolves. Through one man a family stays united and flourishing. God has made you to generate the prosperity of a people in a time such as this. Interjecting the fact that history is made up of two words: His – story which is God's story about events in an individual lives.

I wish you a great journey in your lifetime but far much more that the chronicles of your life shall reflect His story as He originally planned at the end of the day. May your life today reveal the story He wrote about you before you were born, His-story shall make you a blessing and put a smile in the heart of God. Dare to study His word, to align to His will and make His ways, yours. Daring to delight God makes the world smile.

Paul the apostle, a man through whom God revealed the different facets of grace through his epistles, was himself a specimen of the subject. A proven murderer of New Testament saints, whose life being turned around to become a protector, an educator and a teacher of the New Testament Covenant revealed a key insight of grace. In II Corinthians 12:9 the Lord God speaks of His grace being sufficient for Paul.

> *And he said unto me, My grace is sufficient for thee:*
> *for my strength is made perfect in weakness. Most*
> *gladly therefore will I rather glory in my infirmities,*
> *that the power of Christ may rest upon me.*

II Corinthians 12:9

This reveals that the strength of grace perfectly sheds light on its true nature with the backdrop of weakness. This gift of grace equates the gift of Christ whose death on the cross has given the weakened human race ability to be restored and perform above the expectations of man. Dismantled by the fallen nature, the devil's dismissal from heaven reduced him to the lowest status of creatures, exchanging his position for Adam's high profile nature. For Adam who was in the high class of God's glory, fell to the devil's lowest point. The devil took the privileges of Adam to become the prince and the power of the air, far above his original fallen state. This created an unspeakably weakened human nature. However, by the goodness and the mercies of God, Jesus reserved this trend by sending the devil back to his lower ebb and brought man back to his original estate and even much more further and above. Far above principalities and powers and thrones and dominion, we are seated with Christ – God's grace. This incredible mystery of God's love produced grace as the epitome of living power, excelling above the devil's principalities and powers.

For Jesus to tell Paul that my grace is sufficient is to say, "You are so highly established in a performance-strength that it makes your weaknesses irrelevant. This is why God can take foolish things of this world to confound the wise, weak things to confound the things that are mighty; the based things and things despised, to bring to nothing the echelon of pomposity that terrorized the human race over the ages (I Corinthians 1:26-29). God's grace is *THAT* powerful. This incredible truth of grace, revealed to Paul, carried him through all the stages of his mandate.

In II Corinthians 4:8-9 God reveals the toughness of grace.

- We are troubled on every side, yet not distressed
- Perplexed, but not in despair
- Persecuted, but not forsaken
- Cast down, but not destroyed

In this writing the strength of grace and its ability to lift us up above failure is revealed. It makes you a multi-successful personality with an enduring shock absorber that preserves the glory, the vision and the destiny revealed through purpose in each individual person. Through the given grace of God (to as many as receive it) we are sentenced to flourish and are packaged to fulfill that which only God can achieve through a man.

> *For all things are for your sakes that the abundant grace might through the thanksgiving of many redound to the glory of God. For which cause we faint not; but though our outward man perish, yet the inward man is renewed day by day. For our light affliction, which is but for a moment, worketh for us a far more exceeding and eternal weight of glory; While we look not at the things which are seen, but at the things which are not seen: for the things which are seen are temporal; but the things which are not seen are eternal.* **II Corinthians 4:15-18**

In conclusion, grace makes very light the afflictions which were once impossible to bear. Challenges designed to annihilate people of vision, we survive resulting in the most incredible success stories ever told, with a kind of salvation that angels look into with amazement. Every individual person on this journey can handle and survive anything contrary to the direction of progress because of grace. If God's grace can reduce shame and reproach to excelling honor and glory, then we can all say, "I can do all things through Christ who strengthens me"; in other words, "I can do all things through grace that works for me!" The goodness of this success story is that the grace of God that brings salvation and extreme transformation has appeared to all men (Titus 2:11).

To Gideon, God expressed His loving kindness and Old Testament grace, calling him a mighty man of valor in his weakest natural state. This pronouncement of God's word became the reality of his life, making him into a mighty man of valor. This means that grace allows you to become a person with greater excellence than before. This grace was valid only to Gideon. Just one man enjoyed that moment of favor. On the contrary in the New Testament we all get to enjoy the momentous outpouring of the nature of God into man, called the grace of our Lord Jesus Christ. May every individual person on his journey to destiny, fall into the hands of the Most High God who gives grace to excel exceedingly, abundantly, above all we can think. Whereas in the Old Testament momentary grace needed for a specific assignment was given to certain individuals; in the New Testament as many as believe in Christ enjoy the limitless status of God's abundant grace in the cradle of His abundant life. Grace is your empowerment to excel at all times in the purpose for which you were born. It enables you please God. Enjoy the journey.

CHAPTER 7:

TIMING

For every power of one, there is the power of time.

The story of Gideon and the transformation of his life overflowing into the deliverance of his people cannot be admired without discussing the time in which things began to turn around for him. To truly appreciate a positive shift is to have a reflection of the situation surrounding the circumstance, which necessitated the change.

Judges 6:1-10 is the account of a sad story in which God's people were dominated by evil as a result of their rebellion against His will. The original purpose of God's design for mankind, to be made in His image and likeness, is for Him to work and walk in fellowship with us. The Creator and the creature were purposed to work together in deep fellowship; in other words, man was made to be in interdependent with God and not the reverse. Obedience to God's laws and principles create safety, protection and great covering. Disobedience to His will sends signals of rebellion and ultimately open doors to evil and disaster. God is light and every natural thing we see is a product of light. Staying in fellowship with God is to stay within His sovereign, covering light with limitless resources for fruitfulness and relevance. Israel reversed the trend by rebellion therefore separating themselves from the light of God and the covering of His grace. The good news about God is how merciful, loving and caring He is. He quickly receives our repentance and instantly continues His previous work of love, grace and empowerment as if rebellion never happened.

The Bible says, "Your sins I forgive and will remember them again no more" (Jeremiah 31:34). Every individual that walks on this earth needs to know the goodness of God as well as understand the pain in the principle of independence from God. The timing of God coming to the aid of Israel couldn't be anymore perfect. Even 24 hours later could have been disastrous and 24 hours earlier could also have reduced the impact of the great change heaven was about to bring upon Israel based on the compassion of God and His ability to forgive and restore. Gideon's people cried unto God, obviously asking Him for mercy in desperation. God then sends a prophet to Israel to explain what they were experiencing. After peace was established between God and His people, the Angel of the Lord was sent as well.

Timing is everything.

> *He hath made every thing beautiful in his time: also he hath set the world in their heart, so that no man can find out the work that God maketh from the beginning to the end.* **Ecclesiastes 3:11**

If He has made everything beautiful in HIS time, then the natural time is subject to the divine time. Further more, the natural Kronos time is made fruitful when it receives from God's Spirit-time. Without the manifestation of heaven's time into the earth, our natural time frames have no prosperity. This is to say, God created the natural time as vehicle for spirit time and purpose to be carried into the earth, for the benefit of both God's perfect will and man's fruitfulness. I therefore dare to say, unless our natural time tables are in partnership with heaven's time tables, vain do we live on the earth. Vanity is therefore the result of a human time spent on this earth in absolute separation from God's time table spiritually. He has made all things beautiful in His time, not in our time. To the extent that we place a demand on His time tables is to the dimension that we prosper effectively. This is to say, unless we marshal our will power to submit to His decisions, we walk carelessly and recklessly, having nothing to offer our generation.

Sensitivity to the times and seasons of God, therefore is imperative to productive leadership and victorious directions. He makes all things beautiful in His time, which infers that beauty, gladness, fulfillment and contentment are in the hands of God's time. Find out God's time – you will locate His purpose. When you connect to His purpose, the blessings of His time will release beauty upon all that which concerns you.

The scripture continues to say, in Ecc 3:11b that He sets the world in their hearts. This amazing statement is effectively saying, that God created the heart of a leader potentially big enough to absorb the world, possess the world, direct the world and rule the world. We are able therefore to have global impact in our life time if the capable heart, in the hands of God is allowed to conceive heaven's plans and not the earthly logical conclusions. Dominion is imperative. We are able to be fruitful, multiply, replenish, subdue and possess dominion over all the works of the hand of God, but this incredible world-changing ability is contingent on how much heaven's vision can be thrust into your heart and how much willingness to follow through, you can put on the table. This is to say, the package of vision and destiny in a leader's world is simile to a negotiation table, in a corporate boardroom setting. As businessmen exchange money for goods and services, we put our will to obey God's plans on the table, to receive unbelievable packages of God's dreams, visions and universal plans in our hearts. In other words, we put our hearts and our willingness on the divine plan to receive the handshake of God's favor that brings us into His potent dreamland of exclusive breakthroughs, for victorious endings. Life in this world, is designed to reflect purpose from heaven. Your decision to walk the divinely planned pathway is like meeting God at the bargaining table where greatness is transferred from Him into the earth through your human vessel. Covenant greatness consequently is born with a decisive drive for impact and leadership glories.

It is a valuable connection to have with God when we yield our life to the Master's call and business culture. He makes us into the phenomenon worth referring to as a success story, for many generations, so long as the earth remains.

In the year 2007, leaving Aberdeen, Scotland to Seattle, Washington, I was surprisingly not able to get onto the flight, because I was told, the check in counter was closed. Connecting my flight from Holland would have been a serious challenge if I was to miss the flight from Scotland. As much as I could say that I was late for the flight, it felt much more as if I was in the middle of a battle with destiny. With my friend we began to pray for a breakthrough. Suddenly, the flight manageress came and mentioning my name, told me to follow her. As she frantically bulldozed her way through security, she instructed me to follow tightly after her and give nobody else my attention except her. *She sternly said,*

"I stopped the airplane so that you can get on board!"

Entering the plane all eyes of the passengers and the flight attendants were on me, as to see, for whose sake was the flight so seriously interrupted, as if there was an expectation for me to apologize to destiny. When I arrived in Amsterdam, I met a gentleman from the Ukraine, who was then the pastor of the largest church in Europe. As we chatted about life, issues, vision and leadership, he said to me, "Emmanuel, I feel like inviting you as

a guest speaker to our annual conference, six months from now."
He further said, "The strange thing is that we already have all
our guest speakers booked and ready to go." That is to say, they
needed no more additional speakers, but he somehow felt very
impressed to invite me anyway. Humbled by this gesture, I made
a mental note not to take this invitation seriously, especially,
when he said that all their speakers were already set. Two weeks
to the conference, I had it in my mind to let him know that I
couldn't make the trip yet was however thankful for the invitation. I was not able to send the email for unknown reasons.

Suddenly I got a very strong email from this gentleman stat-
ing, "I can hardly sleep without thinking of you coming to the
conference. Please get your ticket and come. You must come!"
In my meditation thereafter, I felt the peace and the release
from the Holy Spirit that this was a God-moment. I opened
the morning session, on the second day of the conference, in an
atmosphere of such a great presence of God with approximately
25,000 delegates in attendance, with a message themed: *The
Movement of the Holy Spirit" (Gen 2:2).*

Later on that evening as it were, I felt pinned to sit in the
green room as if arrested by eternity knowing very well that
conference had already been in motion with all delegates in the
auditorium. Across the greenroom where I was a gentlemen, his
wife and two sons, were sitting on the couch, minding their
own business, as if waiting under on an eternal instruction. The
Holy Spirit impressed upon me to ask the gentleman this question, "Sir, what would happen to your father's organization, if

he would die today?" Before he could answer that question, the Holy Spirit said, "Tell Him, that he needed his father's blessing urgently!" Before he could answer the second question, the Holy Spirit said, "Tell him that he, as the second born, is the ordained heir to the presidency of this cooperation after his father according to the will of God.

Remember all this while, I barely knew who this gentleman was, except once seeing him on television. Obviously as stunned as I was about these three questions to a strange man, he and his family looked very arrested by the moment. Little did I know how seriously they took this event. I found out months later that Mr. Matthew Crouch flew from Kiev, the capital of Ukraine, where this event was, straight to his parents in California and sought their blessing.

Prior to their arrival they had a phone call from another a prominent man of God who presented the same message, only his was a warning dream narrative of how precarious it is, for him not to miss the visitation of God for his life. Obviously Matthew and Laurie were walking in a massive, divine time-line ordination. Within 24 hours after this, the late Prophet Kim Clement called them with an urgent word from God, saying to Matthew, "You need your father's blessing now!" On arrival to his father's house in Los Angeles, he narrated his experience within the past 36 hours, of his obvious encounter with providence as it relates to serving the demands of God for his life and Trinity Broadcasting Network, with no personal agenda. This unexpected interference of God in His life, was a major plan-changer for his life and family. Thriving so well on his own, without TBN in the movie industry, Matthew had to fervently abandon his own agenda for life in the humility of purpose to submit to God in heaven and his parents, the late Paul and Jan Crouch. It is an amazing story to be told when purpose and time collide on a chosen vessel, in the earth realm. There comes and obvious activation of creation that assembles behind the manifestation of such sons and people of God. I pray today that the will of God will not be intimidated in your hands, but rather thrive through you when you yield your own mandate to the call of God into leadership. There is nothing more fulfilling than this. The proof that you are connected to your timing in God is the in practical evidence of everything around you that get out of control for God to take control. Timing can never be ignored when it comes to the ultimate purpose of God for a life, a nation, an organization and a generation. May you be arrested by the sovereign hand of God to the glory of God, in the land of the living. Success in God is knowing His will, yielding to His will and running with His will without regrets.

In this encounter, his father Paul Crouch Sr. asked Matt, "Do you ever see the day that you would come to serve and lead this organization?" In his humble response to his father's request, h "Papa, do you ever see me coming to serve you to lead this organization according to your decision?" His father's response was, "Yes I do, absolutely!"

Today Mr. Matthew and Laurie Crouch chair this great and successful broadcasting network having unprecedented impact on the human race, to say the least. By this heaven's vision which was born through Paul and Jan crouch in the earth, has transcended into the leadership of the next generation, with drive, purpose, vision and illumination for the next dimension of impact on the human race globally. The incredible plan of God for every leader has trans-generational dimensions. To the event that a sovereign plan of God misses a strategic link, is to the effect that the earth loses a major blessing. It is highly appreciated to say the least, that whereas the founders of TBN, Paul and Jan Crouch, endured the pains of building this great network with the sacrifice of their lives, soul, with the discipline of faith and devotion to God, the destiny is in the hands of a formidable leadership of Matthew and Laurie Crouch. The second generation of a long journey of global influence, impact and direction without fail. The journey is on under the governing covering of the mighty hand of God, all through eternity.

The command of Kingdom purpose and vision is in flight by prophecy and so shall it be for every individual who dares to dare the plan of God for their lives by belief and faith!

If I had missed the flight from Scotland to Holland, I wouldn't have met the gentleman who invited me to Kiev, to meet brother Matthew. People and circumstances that God uses to connect our time tables to His will are as important as the ultimate goal. Such angels of help are a unique gift of God inter-planted in our journeys on this earth. The value of that season of life would have been removed but for that angel of visitation that brought us together for such a divine cause as this. If missing one person can make you lose out, then meeting another person can make you gain. It takes the favor of providence to work on your behalf, so long as you continue to trust in Him on your exclusive journey of leadership and purpose.

Believe that all it takes for God's mercy to move on your behalf is for another angel to connect you to another person for recovery. The absence of this kind of help produces emptiness of life. Heaven's networking of key people providentially in the earth makes progressive because of the profitable fruits produced. For that matter, missing that divine appointment in Holland would have been a breach of divine timing and consequential to the possible obstruction and probable abortion of a major divine plan of God with strategic time sensitivity. The *mismanagement of timing* in God's world and in the life we see today, is the reason for missing the mark and sometimes into the most irrecoverable and expensive dimensions so long as the earth remains. God's will is however ultimately done but if His prime time programs are missed they come with a deep price package to restoration. My prayer is to always let God order your steps so you can be seasoned with His timing, because out of His timing comes every provision, help and the master plan.

Timing is a composite package in attaining God's willful plans and expectations. The interwoven dynamics of perfect plans of heaven for the earth in designated time schedules, create the platform of unprecedented results and victories. May the Lord arise on your behalf to connect you in perfect time to His perfect will, meeting strategic people with **designated divine agendas. I see the fresh breath of God. I see the fresh anointing and a renewed grace from God upon you to recover from any time-loss by an accelerated act** of providence for your success. For every appointed time you missed in the past, valuable and purposeful opportunities might have eluded you. May God therefore double your speed to perfect His timing and profit for your life. I pray for the hand of God to sustain your ascendancy and manifestation with an unfailing favor from heaven. The Lord of all purpose and destinies who is the architect of glory, is waiting at the finish line with open arms to embrace you with an eternal kiss of satisfaction, gratification, joy, fulfillment, reward and congratulations!

You are an exclusive personality in the master plans of God's leadership strategies. Lead well with the understanding of heaven's time tables for your life and generation. Connect the dots with your obedience and sacrifice as a true leader. Endeavor to take advantage of your time for in it holds your relevance to heaven and the earth.

For every power of one, there is the power of time.

He make all things beautiful in His time!

May the reading of this book be a simile of a divine encounter between you and the Lord for your circumstance. God comes to build, heal, restore and advance. He is an advocate of prosperity and to everybody who desires to let go their handicaps by faith and lay hold on God's provision and direction; it therefore requires a yielded vessel to experience the empowerment of one man.

> *Remember the former things of old: for I am God, and there is none else; I am God, and there is none like me, Declaring the end from the beginning, and from ancient times the things that are not yet done, saying, My counsel shall stand, and I will do all my pleasure.*   **Isaiah 46:9-10**

TIMING

It is often said, "timing is everything" and it certainly does influence everything. On the fourth day of creation God made time. Out of the seven days He made time to be the pivotal calibration between the first three days and the last three days, creating time as a silver thread that activates the purpose of everything created in the seven days. Time provokes the chromosomes of perfection in everything under God's perfect will. He makes all things beautiful in *His* time. Many times we want God to function within our time-frame but the best deals of life are always found within the orbit of God's perfect timing. All things fall into place *except* the wrong things. The perfection of God's time table connecting to our purpose gives us the trump card we need to achieve our highest and our most ever to be dreamed of. The handicap of man is to think, "If God loves me, He will do what I say," but the truth is, if God loves you He will do for you what He has planned. "Why doesn't God tell me everything?"

Well He doesn't have to because you will not understand based on the classifications of the power of handicap, which limits our understanding of divine plans and purposes. Gideon said, "Where are all the miracles that our fathers spoke about?" Bordering on doubt, God turned things around at just the right time and Gideon became the chosen man, whose valiance (as an act of God through him) turned around the story of impoverishment and averted the holocaust of His generation. This is the power of one man in the hands of a purpose driven and loving God.

CHAPTER 8:

PURPOSE AND COUNSEL

All people go through controversies but how can they succeed and prevail without counsel? The tragedy of life is in people dying without purpose. It is also reflected in being cut off in the midst of fulfilling your purpose in your prime time. Counsel from God therefore secures, protects, and prevents this anomaly. The scriptures say that to subvert a man in his course the Lord approveth not (Lamentations 3:36). Meaning it is not the desire of God for an individual to be aborted in the process of God's time-line for him or her. This is why Heaven makes counsel available in the process of your time, to the glory of God.

Purpose can be defined as: the reason why something exists

and is created. Purpose is also the subject at hand or the point of issue. To have a purpose is to establish your relevance and identity in the earth. It is also the package of God's insightfulness about you and your role in His master plan revealed and directed by providence. Purpose cannot be found; it is given when you stay in alignment with the pathways of God and in His presence. It creates an awareness of who you are and what you were designed for so that you can become the delight of many generations. Purpose makes you shine in the midst of your generation. It makes you productive in your time of life.

Proverbs 20:18 declares that every purpose is established by counsel and with good advice you make war. The difference between advice and counsel is whereas the former is derived out of the experience and opinion of men, the latter is out of the depths of God's wisdom. Counsel has more eternal roots and sustenance than advice. Whereas advice can be interchangeable as seasons come and go, counsel is constantly being born out of God and His inspiration. The value of your purpose demands the depths of counsel.

> *O Lord, Thou art my God; I will exalt Thee, I will praise Thy name; for thou hast done wonderful things; Thy counsels of old are faithfulness and truth.*

> **Isaiah 25:1**

The success story of Gideon was a result of the counsel of the Angel of the Lord, by whose instructions he followed to go to his father's house and pull down the ungodly grove (Judges 6:25-

31). There is a significance to everybody's success story derived from this event. There are certain ungodly inspirations from family lineages which prohibit people from being the individuals God has purposed and established them to be. These could be bad omens, curses, ungodly altars, groves, high places, totem poles, ancient tokens, stones, etc., which are based on unclean covenants made with individuals of the past in family lineages. These become strongholds carrying spiritual interferences to the smooth sailing advancements according to the will of God for your life.

How could Gideon have ever known the importance of destroying such groves even when his own father had no clue of how devastating it was? Certain generations hold on to some ungodly beliefs covered by beautifully packaged stories yet underneath could be hidden drawbacks and bloodline treachery. This kind of antagonistic spiritual mystery could have been the reason for many years as to why Gideon and his family were considered small and absolutely irrelevant. They were not created to be so, but the beliefs of the descendants opened the doors for unclean spirits. The power of counsel gave Gideon the key to root out and destroy this hidden mystery. Gideon took ten of his servant men and did as the Lord said to him. The number '10' signifying responsibility; was the beginning of the mighty valiance of this young man who used to be timid and irrelevant in obscurity, now beginning his journey into the limelight. The power of one man is able to abolish and bring to an end the devastation of a generation; in one day, one season, one lifetime.

This in turn enables the freeing of the past, present, and future from pain, chaos and myopia.

> *Then Gideon took ten men of his servants, and did as the Lord had said unto him: and so it was, because he feared his father's household, and the men of the city, that he could not do it by day, that he did it by night. And when the men of the city arose early in the morning, behold, the altar of Baal was cast down, and the grove was cut down that was by it, and the second bullock was offered upon the altar that was built.*
>
> *And they said one to another, Who hath done this thing? And when they inquired and asked, they said, Gideon the son of Joash hath done this thing. Then the men of the city said unto Joash, Bring out thy son, that he may die: because he hath cast down the altar of Baal, and because he hath cut down the grove that was by it. And Joash said unto all that stood against him, Will ye plead for Baal? will ye save him? he that will plead for him, let him be put to death whilst it is yet morning: if he be a god, let him plead for himself, because one hath cast down his altar.* **Judges 6:27-32**

Contention ensued after the discovery of the ungodly altar for the first time which positively provoked Gideon's father who previously had always subjugated himself to the servitude of this small god, an altar of satan. Now he had boldness like never before to agree with the destruction of this lying spirit which had caused small mindedness, timid-thinking tendencies and great failure in their family. This satanic god, literally the killer of their prosperity, was overthrown by the counsel of God.

Since everybody's purpose is unique, counsel can be specifically designed to meet the requirements to advance purpose. Counsel is a pillar of truth which never fails, so in all thy getting, get understanding (Proverbs 4:7). This scripture opens your spirit to seek counsel from Holy Spirit inspired people, books, resources, etc. In other words, whereas counsel is perennial, perpetual and everlasting, producing consistent results; advice is annual and therefore much more short-lived. Advice is the product of the light of the experience of men; counsel is the product of the light of God. This is the reason why Proverbs 21:30 states that there is no wisdom nor understanding nor counsel against the Lord. This refers to how the limited advice and understanding of the wisest man cannot prevail against God, who obviously functions in the highest level of glory. Having said that, God has no counsel to give because He is the counsel. When you seek God's counsel, you have Him working for you. Therefore in the multitude of counsel that is to say, in the abundance of godly, matters are settled.

It is my prayer that you locate the right counsel for your purpose driven life to be fueled to maximum productivity. God loves everyone He creates and favors as many as desire His input, His presence and His will. If God can do it for this one,

He can do it for you. By the advice of his tribe, Gideon's father ignorantly built an evil spirited altar of worship because that was the experience of their descendants in those days. It produced negative results and diminutive cultures of failure without his knowing. As limited as the grove was, it took nothing short of the sovereign counsel of God to turn things around and establish Gideon and the entire family as the overcoming leaders they were born to be.

It is therefore important to note that the power of ignorance in the life of potential champions can produce cultures of failure; as the scripture say that due to lack of knowledge, My people perish (Hosea 4:6). I pray deliverance from ignorance and haughty innocence. May counsel find you today and deliver you from what you were not born to be and establish you as that one person with keys of breakthrough for many generations. This is your time and this is your day! Enjoy your life in the orbit of God's counsel prepared for you before the foundations of the world; *The power of one man in the hands of God.*

CHAPTER 9:

SAMUEL

Born to a frustrated mother called Hannah who was barren for many years, found favor in the sight of the Lord. Samuel was dedicated unto God's divine purpose to become the one man whose leadership determined the emergence of a new social order, in a generation that once upon a time languished under God's disfavor. Hannah received the blessing of a male child whose name in the Hebrew means, "name of God." Samuel was born in a time when Israel had gone through a series of corrupt priestly leadership resulting in painful defeats by their enemies the Philistines. The society had become subjugated to godlessness, secular humanism and corrupt moral values. It is amazing the influence of leadership and how much it can solve problems or create them.

The study of the subject of leadership has proven it to be a womb out of which fortunes and misfortunes are brewed, victories and failures are made, depression and impressions revealed and limitless advancements are birthed. Leadership is also the key to making crooked paths straight, smoothing rough edges, reducing mountains into molehills and filling valleys for a leveled pathway. Leadership is the machinery that creates atmospheres for others to discover their purpose in God. It is a valuable key that should never be found in wrong or immature hands because of the magnitude of its power in the lifetime of a person, a people and a generation. Leadership creates the platform for the unborn to fail or succeed. *I pray for God's wind of correction to blow over all in leadership and remove failure tendencies and establish the tapestry of glorious excellence with atmospheres of blissful encounters and dominion!* The scriptures say that in the days when Samuel was born God had become so distant from His people that there was no word from God, ever.

> *And the child Samuel ministered unto the Lord before Eli. And the word of the Lord was precious in those days; there was no open vision.* **1 Samuel 3:1**

It is usually said that *God has walked away from His people,* but the truth rather is people walk away from their God and therefore distant themselves from the true blessing of their loving Creator and Father. Some know the story of the prodigal son who strayed away from his father's world into destruction but returned in repentance, reconnecting to the glory of his father and continuing in prosperity. The nation out of which Samuel was born experienced great defeats in spite of the application of God's principles at war.

It is essential to understand that applying the principles of God may produce limited results and in some cases no results, if they are not done God's way.

It takes God to make His principles work, not man. Mankind and his principles work together and fail within the framework of man's limitations but God's ordinances are as strong as His person. Choose God as your relative and abide by His principles for a long lasting cycle of blessings and good results in time and eternity. The devastation of the previous leadership in the days of Samuel set the stage for his relevance. The nation was the same but they produced far much more results when God changed the leadership. Samuel the new leader brought in new dimensions of conquest and recovery.

In 1 Samuel 7:1-17 we see the exclusive grace of a leader in God's favor turning around a national crisis into an unbelievable success story in his lifetime. The Ark of the Covenant of God which represented the statutory Covenant of God's manifest presence in the national affairs, was brought back after being captured by the Philistines. The previous two chapters revealed graphically the mishandling of God's glory by previous leadership. It also showed how effective God is to fight His own battles such as the scenario with Gideon's father and the family shrine which could not fight for itself. God is timeless, ageless and self-existent. He has no beginning and no end. He is the Most High to whom nothing is impossible therefore by whom all great successes are achieved. He is the only omnipotent, omnipresent and omniscient God Almighty from whom all blessings, strength, counsel and vitality flow; from whom comes also love unspeakable, grace unimaginable and power unfathomable. Yahweh is His name. Gideon did exploits as one man in the counsel of God in his days, so did Samuel in his time and so shall it be in your days, even as you read this book.

Samuel's leadership initiatives gathered Israel for a national reconciliation ceremony in Mizpah. With the influence of Samuel's effective leadership, Israel denounced their wrong and sinful cultural values and walked away from paganism, giving their hearts back to the true God who Samuel represented. In their appeal to Samuel to pray for them, asking God's mercy and forgiveness, we learn the lessons of the power of intercession through the prayer of any person who has favor with God. Not only does God answer genuine heart felt prayers, but He even so much more responds to those who have found good will in His sight through their steadfast faithful alliance with Him.

Developing a relationship with God is very important in the life of everyone who has what it takes to make a difference. The power of a person to shift the direction of a people is derived out of His relationship with God. The key is the God-factor. Samuel's relationship with God was deep and therefore very trusted, so much so that the people believed in his interventional plea on their behalf. The power of one to make inroads in magnitudes can also be found in how much the people trust in their leader's veracity. The proof of his capability to turn things around was not in Samuel's acclamation of God, but in his deeds and stately stature.

A man must live in deeds not in words.

The significance of a person to lead and change testimonies should be in the proof of his or her faith, by works and the sustainability of the fruitful principles of leadership. Samuel engaged God through his sacrifice and prayers, that in the event of an unannounced attack of the Philistines as before, the power of God exposed their enemies by great thunder right before their eyes. That is how possible it is for a man to provoke the power of God on behalf of his generation. This also is a clear revelation of how dear Samuel was to the heart of God. It is possible for God to be attached to a man in such a loving capacity that attracts the admiration of many. May you find a place in God like this. Samuel was therefore considered as the trusted prophet in his days. The result of his victory established the stone memorabilia named *Ebenezer* with the inscription, "Hitherto has the Lord helped us" (I Samuel 7:12). It is possible for a man to have such high favor with God to the benefit of an entire generation. This is to say, whereas the whole nations could not get God's attention, one man in the nation did and brought a desired result for the multitude through the office of *one man*. This is true favor. The category of this kind of leadership is relevant for our time.

May God raise many such as this in every nation. The minimum of even one such a person, in every nation of the earth, could be enough to bring heaven to earth. God can deliver by many, by a few or even by just *one* who dares to stay in covenant with the Lord. Through all the generations of the human race, the breakthroughs of the many have been found in the hands of the few or in some cases, *the one in question.*

I Samuel 7:14 records a monumental proof of the how much restoration one person can bring to a lost generation. In all the days of the leadership of Samuel, the Philistines were subdued and could not come near the coastline of the land because the hand of God became a wall of protection over the land. It also states that the land and property captured by the enemy was restored and Israel was totally delivered from the grips of oppression.

> *And the cities which the Philistines had taken from Israel were restored to Israel, from Ekron even unto Gath; and the coasts thereof did Israel deliver out of the hands of the Philistines. And there was peace between Israel and the Amorites.*   **I Samuel 7:14**

The power of one man is revealed through the hands of a strategic leader who understood his purpose and made due diligence of his responsibility, both to God and the citizens of his land. You have all it takes to stand between chaos and order, between failure and success and between depravity and productivity. It's wonderful to have a team, but if there is none, it's much more beautiful to be the life-wire and the originator of the right kind. Great governments stand tall by the strength of formidable leaders. The power of one man in the hand of a trusted God brings glory to worlds of generations. *Can we find such a person in you?* I say yes. It is in everybody who dares to submit their life into the hands of the Lord. *Is it possible to achieve such greatness?* The answer is that with God on your side, He is more than the majority in the natural, therefore:

ONE + GOD = DOMINION & REDEMPTION

Bring a smile to the world you came to find and after your departure from this earth may it be known that a leader once sojourned and left indelible footprints of remarkable results. I pray you become the irreplaceable one eternity made you to be. May your potential begin to awaken the sleeping giant within you! Rise up and lead! Arise, shine, for your light is come.

CHAPTER 10:

QUEEN ESTHER

The proof of an effective leader's purpose is revealed in the fulfillment of the vision. Having said that, the choice of every leader in his function is always connected to divine time sensitivity. The composite dynamics of a person's time-frame is made up of the content of each season in their life. Esther was an orphan who found grace in the sight of her uncle Mordecai. Both captives in the reign of King Ahasuerus of Persia, a large kingdom which expanded present day India into Ethiopia marked by 127 provinces, regions or states. The back drop of every success story draws attention to the relevance of such a person's role in life.

There is such a thing as *backstage leadership* in which no one sees and no one knows except God and you. The backstage is usually the last point before center stage. On the center stage of this great kingdom was a queen called Vashti whose beauty, splendor, and grace unfortunately built in her a stately arrogance, pride, and insubordination. In the event of her continuous growth in this unacceptable gesture of queenship, she was suddenly removed from office because her attitude endangered the marital success story of Persia. So long as a leader becomes a point of reference, it is always imperative to behave wisely. To whom much is given, much is required. Conclusively, as much as could not be said about the details of Vashti, the stage had appropriately been prepared for the emergence of a new queen whose fulfillment granted her name to be the title of one of the books in the Holy Bible.

Esther was beautiful, stately, and yet graced so much more with favor. Certain giftings in life are considered *master keys,* which are able open distinct doors everywhere and anytime. Favor is one of those gifts in life. It will take you where no one else can take you and do for you what even the government of a nation cannot do to help. The endowment of favor for Esther was very needful because she was a Jew whose native roots disqualified her from being part of the pageantry team of the government of Persia. As it was in the life of Gideon, the underdog for the job, so it was for Esther. On the day of her presentation, she found favor before the king who loved her and crowned her as queen and first lady. Unbeknownst to her, the response to the call as queen was making God's eternal distinctive plan to preserve and protect her people in their days of captivity in Persia, a reality. Strategically planned in advance, the annihilation of the Jews was a conspiracy, which would have been the first holocaust, ahead of Adolph Hitler. This is noteworthy to every one person that is to be a key for a generation. There is so much more to the purpose of your life in the eyes of God, than you could ever know. At that time, Esther was in a state of celebration and blissfulness as queen of the most powerful empire on the planet.

POSITIONED BY PRESSURE

Positioned by pressure, Esther took responsibility and understood that her role had changed from being a first lady to a deliverer. Sometimes, there is an unveiling of your purpose under the sudden pressures of life. Being clueless as to what to do, can be the best thing in discovering your purpose reason for living. If there was any tangible reason for her existence, it was discovered through the pressure that made her put her life on the line. The *Power of One*, as the title of the book, always requires putting your life on the line. It will cost you everything. It can demand the sacrifice of everything that is necessary for every singular discovery of one's strategic positioning to produce results of the divine calling; *positioned by pressure*.

The dirt around gold is removed and the polishing of the gem produces priceless value. Pressure will repackage you and deploy you just like a diamond cutter who gets the right position to produce a priceless diamond piece. The position of pressure sets you up, as well as sets the stage for you to be distinguished and different, so as to be accepted as the only one person for the job. Esther said, "If I perish, I perish" (Esther 4:16). In other words she was saying, "I'm going full steam ahead. I'm gathering myself together and putting everything on the line. I'm going for it!"

This was a statement of great faith knowing very well that the only authority that could possibly help her was God. It was a one chance, "make or break" decision. Thomas Edison took that one chance as did Martin Luther King, George Washington, Bill Gates, Mark Zuckerberg, Steve Jobs and the list goes on. It has been proved that under God's grace everyone who said, *"If I perish, I perish," has* never perished. Such positions transition you through the ordinary average to extraordinary distinction. It is almost like a cliff of destiny you have to jump over. With the wrong perspective, many fall trying to make it in their own strength, but with the right vision and partnership with God, many make it with clarion success.

It is imperative therefore for every one person on such a highway of destiny to learn the management of pressure. It must be managed, can be managed, and *should* be managed to the benefit of all. Pressure can turn sour when mismanaged and mishandled. As destructive as fire can be, it is most productive when properly managed; the same is true for pressure. May the Holy Spirit put into your hands today the skill and the keys to manage your pressure knowing for a fact that it is part of the creation process; not a judgment but an asset.

Pressure has nothing to do with sin in your life, nor righteousness in its holiest presence on your life. It is the journey which every person that comes on this earth walks through. To every great journey there are rough roads and crooked paths which characterize the vision and classify the purpose of your mandate. The power of a willing vessel fully persuaded as Esther was, in the midst of humongous pressure, always brings the best out of everyone who dares to be the best in their challenging times, having put their faith in God. As pressure on a pregnant woman increases with pain during childbirth, to announce the birthing of a dignified life, so is pressure the proof of the final stages of a long crisis, about to embrace solutions and victory.

The proper management of this pressure on Esther was to the effect that she went on a three-day fast, praying and seeking the help of God. She received this help by way of the endowment of unspoken favor from the king whose scepter was stretched towards her, with the offer of up to half of his kingdom and more. The connection between Esther's stand of faith and the favor she received from God through the king, blocked the death assignment of her uncle Mordecai. It reversed the judgment of death back to the architect of the assignment, Haman, a vizier in the Persian empire under King Ahasuerus. It put in writing the reversal of the constitutional clause that spearheaded the annihilation of all Jews in the Persian empire, extending from Ethiopia all the way to present day India. Esther restored and preserved the prophecy of Jewish tribe; she caused Mordecai's coronation and the people of her birth advantaged over their enemies which turned their sorrows into dancing by giving them joy, honor, and a good day to celebrate the kindness of God. It established a historical, annual celebration of the feast of Purim.

The world bows its heart in appreciation to singular voices who look beyond themselves and care more for the advantage of others beyond their own needs. They are the ones who make it happen. It is a life worth living. It is a victory worth having and a contentment worth experiencing. It is worth it all to put a smile on the face of many generations, endless generations and sometimes eternal generations. To imagine that the stand of one leader can throw so much light of hope to brighten eternity makes God's principle of using one person, a joy to embrace. You are that one person who should not be stopped by the disapproval of horizontal relationships simply because God is on your side. You are endorsed by the greatest authority whose glory and presence far outweigh the accolade or the disapproval and discomfort produced by the rejection of *logical thinkers*. You are endorsed and approved by grace as a vessel of mercy in partnership with the only wise God, who knows the end from the beginning, as well as designs the end to the beginning with a proven record of accomplishments.

Expectations create condensed atmospheres of pressure in the mind and in some cases, your spirit. Leadership with strategic dream packages especially in troubled times go through this. Every person called into leadership goes through this pathway of pressure.

STRATEGIES

Many times we look into our personal experience databank for resources or depend on someone else's analysis of the matter while under pressure, but this may not be appropriate for the pressure you are under. There is always a need to discover your own rhythm while under pressure. For instance, King David felt the pressure on the army of Israel that had mounted for 40 days because of the overwhelming dominance of Goliath. Goliath was a tower and mystery of opposition and oppressiveness which outwitted the skills of a highly rated military led by king Saul of Israel. With a determination to handle Goliath as one man, David was faced with choosing the strategy of a previous record in the framework of the armor of King Saul which I consider a, *"same old, same old principle"* or *"that's how it's been, that's how we fought battles in the past,"* the status quo.

It is evident through history that strategies have expiration dates. When their time of good news expires, they are eventually reduced to inspirations but are disqualified to become directives and instructions for the new and unknown which lies ahead. David, in preparation behind the scenes, had a fresh inspiration and strategy for the generation of untold leadership to come. He said, "I have not proved your armor sir. As good as it sounds, there is need to go ahead with what I have just discovered by myself and for myself, which has not failed me yet (I Samuel 17:39).

While standing face to face with Goliath in the valley of Elah and an audience of two army strongholds, their strategies, intelligence armament, and armory and skill, David in the coliseum of military uncertainties and internal wishes intermingled with fear, failure, embarrassment, strength and weakness, made a loud proclamation against Goliath. "I come against you in the name of the God of Israel." This statement settled the case for his strategy not to fail. Having just rejected the strategy of the armor of Saul, he laid hold of the strategy of the name of God behind his slingshot. Goliath came down like the Berlin wall. It was as if the great mountains melted in the presence of God.

> *Oh that thou wouldest rend the heavens, that thou wouldest come down, that the mountains might flow down at thy presence.* **Isaiah 64:1**

God approved and endorsed the power of one man who dared to be original in his thinking by laying hold of the counsel of God for his purpose to be fulfilled. It is the glory of God to conceal strategies but it is the honor of great thinkers, great minds and world changers to seek them out by the help of the Holy Spirit, in great humility with passion to make a difference. It is essential for all readers of this book to take note that there is always a different strategy for every individual whose mandate by providence, is supposed to be on the scene. Discover for yourself, after aligning your destiny to God's plan, the keys He has for you in your package to fulfillment, contentment and victory. So goes the saying, *"there must be a new wine for a new wine skin."*

Pressure has a high propensity of pushing key leaders into

hunger for solutions. It stirs thirst for discovery because of the hopelessness of circumstances in the wake of a great need for deliverance. Those who submit themselves under God ride the waves of contrary winds to connect to infallible solutions, which only God can download to their attentive spirit. There is therefore a thorough need for a sound strategy for every one person, to fulfill his or her mandate gracefully and with lasting results.

Grown and groomed by the obvious predetermined counsel of the Lord into the seat of power, Queen Esther suddenly had to be awakened to the original reason she was created; which was to preserve life, her people and above all, the master plan of God for that time and generations to come.

> *For if thou altogether holdest thy peace at this time,*
> *then shall there enlargement and deliverance arise*
> *to the Jews from another place; but thou and thy*
> *father's house shall be destroyed: and who knoweth*
> *whether thou art come to the kingdom for such a*
> *time as this?* **Esther 4:14**

It is a true saying that due to the lack of full understanding and knowledge of one's purpose, life can be handled carelessly and recklessly. This was so in the life of Vashti who accepted foolishness in her heart and was replaced by Esther. I pray that God takes folly out of our hearts so that we might stay malleable, as the one person chosen for the one relevant assignment, to the benefit of many generations. I pray that God gives you full understanding that you might stay fit in the hands of destiny as that one person chosen for that one relevant assignment, accomplishing all He has ordained for you. The power of one can be a risky proposition, but gratifying when fulfilled.

CHAPTER 11:

VERTICAL & HORIZONTAL PRESSURE

There are expectations from heaven as to your purpose and your calling. These expectations from the Lord are based on what He knows He has put in you and expects of you according to His purpose and predetermined counsel; these are considered as "vertical expectations." There are also "horizontal pressures" as to what society and the natural world expects of you in your place of authority, leadership, position, office, and role. It is very possible and usually the case, that the horizontal pressure from people can attempt to steer you off course from what God created you for. If for any reason, you buy into horizontal pressure, you may have good motives and the desire to produce results but end up in a total collapse. This happens because most don't consider what the purpose or requirements of God are for them, especially when in dire straits. It is almost like a scenario of a pilot that collapses in the cockpit, God forbid, and expecting a cotton farmer who has no clue of aerodynamics to fly a commercial airplane. The desire to take control of the airplane could be right but the pressure on the wrong person to solve that emergency is dangerous. We many times fall short when discerning the counsel of God and in turn create a chain of painful challenges. The most progressive approach to many pressures is to always be in counsel with the Holy Spirit, who is ever ready to guide, help, inspire and direct anyone under pressure, either vertically or horizontally. Pressure from both angles, in the vein of expectation for desired goals, cannot be controlled.

However your passion to get in touch with God is your choice and is under your control, therefore the power of one in the hand of a mysterious God can produce limitless results. If God be *for* you and *with* you and *in* you, then it's amazing what *even* a cotton farmer can do in a cockpit, having no clue how to fly an airplane. He can be inspired by God to do wonders by dropping strategic thoughts into the mind of a willing vessel.

> *For thou wilt light my candle: the LORD my God*
> *will enlighten my darkness. For by thee I have run*
> *through a troop; and by my God have I leaped over*
> *a wall. As for God, his way is perfect: the word of the*
> *LORD is tried : he is a buckler to all those that trust*

in him. For who is God save the LORD? or who is a rock save our God? It is God that girdeth me with strength, and maketh my way perfect. He maketh my feet like hinds' feet, and setteth me upon my high places. He teacheth my hands to war, so that a bow of steel is broken by mine arms. Thou hast also given me the shield of thy salvation: and thy right hand hath held me up, and thy gentleness hath made me great. Thou hast enlarged my steps under me, that my feet did not slip. **Psalm 18:28-36**

CHAPTER 12:

THE EXPEDIENCY
OF COUNSEL

The power of wise counsel and its need on this earth at all times cannot be over-emphasized. Counsel is defined as: the interchange of opinions as to future procedures, consultations, deliberations. It is also an instruction given in directing the judgment or conduct of another. It is considered as one of the cardinal values every single individual needs to become outstanding. The Bible says that every purpose is established by counsel (Proverbs 20:18). Referring to the counsel of the great God that created you, inspirations are downloaded with keys of help which never fail as you fellowship and interact with Him.

Oh lord thou art my God, I will exalt thee, I will
praise thy name for thou has done wonderful things;
thy counsel of old are faithful and true. **Isaiah 25:1**

True counsel is produced and derived from dialogue and deep fellowship; in other words as you grow in your relationship with God, He drops counsel into your spirit concerning the now and the future and how to connect the two with the highest standard you can ever dream of. Job 32:8 says there is a spirit in man and the inspiration of God gives him understanding. This means for every one individual in the hand of God designed to make a difference, there is a need for a divine inspiration to open the understanding of your mind and your spirit as to what you are the best at. Hidden counsels from God can only be received from God and not from universities, educational institutions or professors of the academic industries of the world. The true activity of God within and around the person of His choice for a specific purpose, is revealed in most cases by the stirring and the provocation of great endowments of fulfillment.

In most cases, counsel from God could be dropped into your spirit as a piece of knowledge for witty inventions. It can therefore manifest from the Holy Spirit as a very practical opportunity which has never been discovered before. To everyone else it may be unheard of, but to the chosen recipients it is a fresh wind of possibility. Every sure counsel of the Lord comes with the inspiration of faith for possibility. With God all things are possible. The virgin Mary was visited by an angel named Gabriel for the conception and virgin birth of the Messiah. In her logical deliberation, she questioned the possibility but after yielding to the counsel of God, it became possible for a woman to have no contact with a physical man yet carry a baby in her womb, by the power of the counsel of God through the Holy Spirit. She said, "Be it unto me according to Your word" (Luke 1:38). She went through a transition of doubt into fulfillment by yielding to the divine equation of possibility and counsel. She accepted the call and the mandate came to pass. The power of counsel drives man from obscurity to the limelight. May you accept your call and mandate to be that *one person* chosen to make a difference like nobody else who ever lived before and that may ever live after you.

Psalm 25:14 declares that the secret of the LORD is with them that fear him; and he will shew them His covenant. Wholesome counsel from the Most High teaches you how to profit and will lead you in the way that you should go.

> *Thus saith the LORD, thy Redeemer, the Holy One of*
> *Israel; I am the LORD thy God which teacheth thee*
> *to profit, which leadeth thee by the way that thou*
> *shouldest go.*   **Isaiah 48:17**

As much as God is not a failure, His counsels make you succeed. Life is to be lived according to the original design always in partnership and in covenant with the true God who created the whole earth with His wisdom. May He baptize you in His counsel forever. It is therefore expedient to have the right network around your destiny. In this case, God should be your first network and godly-minded people need to be the inclusion of your second network. Such relationship produces a tapestry of valuable principles which build a firewall of protection, security, preservation and stepping stones for you to excel with.

Mordecai was a very prudent government official working in the king's palace, called Shushan, whose position around Esther as a counselor, guiding her with love, he helped her make the right choices. In addition, with his networking, Mordecai discovered a sophisticated plan to annihilate the Jewish tribe from the earth. Weakened by the supremacy of the plot, he came to the conclusion of utilizing the *power of one* to abort this menace. Esther's name showed up as the only person on the earth, naturally, who could make this happen. Life under God is fascinating, especially when He presents individuals as a solution, different than every person's choice. The fact that God uses one person's availability to do great works is the reason why people come on the scene suddenly without any previous announcement to fulfill a cause. Where was Esther in the incubation of the plot behind the scenes? On the emergence of the scheme came the sudden unveiling of the name *Esther*. It almost sounds like when the enemy presses his button of evil, God releases the inspiration of a much more sophisticated strategy in the power of one, to counter act the enemies plan, so as to keep the divine process uninterrupted.

The revealing of the one person in time of need suggests there must have been a spiritual readiness of an advance knowledge of events before the natural world sees it. It's refreshing to note that God, who sees the end from the beginning of life, presents in the highest form of wisdom, the master piece of fruitful solutions. Such power to have formidable solutions in readiness proves the availability of counsel to everyone that is called for a purpose. Counsel therefore is much more sophisticated and advanced if it is from God; it is the reason why every purpose is established.

> *Without counsel purposes are disappointed: but in the multitude of counselors they are established.*
>
> **Proverbs 15:22**

> *O Lord, thou art my God; I will exalt thee, I will praise thy name; for thou hast done wonderful things; thy counsels of old are faithfulness and truth.*
>
> **Isaiah 25:1**

> *Counsel in the heart of man is like deep water; but a man of understanding will draw it out.*
>
> **Proverbs 20:5**

The verse above reflects that counsel is deeper than advice. Whereas advice reflects the databank of human experience, counsel depicts the unsearchable depths of wisdom, ingenious glory and magnificence in the heart of God, only made available to those who fear God and desire His presence. If without counsel purposes are defeated, then every individual on this planet needs counsel to be relevant. Therefore, let every person called to make a change and to make a difference seek His counsel. It is key to the wise, food for the prudent, life for world changers and a well of joy to achievers.

Unfortunately, Queen Esther was clueless as to what was going on. When contacted on the subject, she explained how impossible it was for her to help because the king was out of time; the machinery of evil had been set in motion and she was debarred from getting access to the king until the execution was over. Esther 4:14 was Mordecai's counsel – one, if thou would altogether hold thy peace at this time, God shall still get the job done by raising somebody else; two, if you fail to help, both you and your father's house shall be annihilated; and three, for what you know, you have been brought into the kingdom for a time such as this.

In life, every person in whose hands the key of solution falls, become eternally irrelevant if they refuse to act or perform according to the will of God. In other words, life is worth living for the very singular reason why you were born. I pray you will not miss your visitation, calling, nor purpose in the time of your life.

Arrested by purpose, Esther gathered herself together and went on a three day fast with a declaration "If I perish, I perish," but I will get this job done! Esther put her life on the line and set the solution process in motion as a singular person. In her solitude Esther stood between eternity and time, between destruction and solution. Being pulled from the expectation vertically she was pressured by human expectation horizontally. So the queen went on a three-day fast with prayer, seeking the right word, in the right will of God, for the right way. Conclusively, she approached the king and found favor to the glory of God; the holocaust was aborted. Haman, the architect of the wickedness was hung. The Jews regained their lost ground and their sorrows were turned into dancing as they entered into the dawning of a new life of hope. This incredible turnaround story earned until today, the Jewish nation an annual celebration of remembrance called, The Feast of Purim. Esther, the story of favor. She was a catalyst in the midst of absolute impossibility and disgrace; *the power of a singular lady in the hand of the infinite God of favor!*

May you ride the waves of the difficult storms around you, as the eagle locks its wings to soar above difficulties. Be the powerful one you were designed to be. It is your time and it is your turn. Lay hold of the most prominent resource available, God Almighty.

CHAPTER 13:

ABSOLUTE OBEDIENCE

O bedience is a very important factor as the *one person* called for a mission. The subject becomes even more strategic because you may have to learn to walk alone, on a pathway designed just for you. Others will bring lots of suggestions but the obedience to the strict directives of the Lord of what you believe needs to be done, should be rest solely in your hands. Obedience is the act or practice of obeying, which can become a lifestyle until the end of your time on this earth. I pray you will stick to what you know you were born to do in all virtuousness and truthfulness, which brings positive gains to life and glory to God.

Obedience to God will give what no one else can give you. It makes you see what no one else can reveal to you and should be considered as journey of life. Abraham for instance had to obey absolutely all the instructions he was given to become the father of faith and of many nations. His first encounter with the Lord was a call for a lifetime change of direction, which required absolute obedience. It was nothing he had ever heard before, ever seen before, ever known before or ever read before, yet he still obeyed. The first command was to depart from his kindred to a land that will be revealed to him. Consider the factor that his destination had no address at that point. God said I will show you where you are to go. Our modern day intelligence tells you to get the entire picture, know where you are going, know how much it will cost you, weigh the cost and prepare adequately. Faith with God doesn't work that way. If He gives you all that information then you are very blessed, but in 99% of the equation you usually you have to trust Him and believe that He knows what He is doing. This is what I call absolute faith, total faith and not looking back on your trust in the Lord.

Romans 4:16-22 speaks about Abraham, who had no alternative but to hope against hope, that he might become the father of many nations. He did not consider the logical weakness of his human anatomy as well as his wife's to have a child at the age of 100.

> *Therefore it is of faith, that it might be by grace; to the end the promise might be sure to all the seed; not to that only which is of the law, but to that also*

which is of the faith of Abraham; who is the father of us all, (As it is written, I have made thee a father of many nations,) before him whom he believed, even God, who quickeneth the dead, and calleth those things which be not as though they were. Who against hope believed in hope, that he might become the father of many nations, according to that which was spoken, So shall thy seed be. And being not weak in faith, he considered not his own body now dead, when he was about an hundred years old, neither yet the deadness of Sarah's womb: He staggered not at the promise of God through unbelief; but was strong in faith, giving glory to God; And being fully persuaded that, what he had promised, he was able also to perform. And therefore it was imputed to him for righteousness. **Romans 4:16-22**

Consider this:

- Abraham believed

- His belief did not stagger

- He was strong in faith and was fully persuaded

For every person who is that *one man* for a generation, must dare to have these attributes and just believe that God is who He is and He can do what He says He can do. For everyone who comes to God must first believe in His existence. God will always meet you at your faith level to bring you to His level. He is kind, gracious, also willing and able to help you succeed. If you are the chosen one for the mandate then He must have put in you all it takes to succeed before you were born. I pray you will dare to be faith-fit and keep your belief fitness with total persuasion and focus on the amazing acts of God who does great things with weak and ordinary people. If HE is able then YOU are able; on the condition that you dare to stay in good fellowship with Him.

Many years later in the history of Abraham, his son Isaac was instructed by God in the days of famine and lack, not to go to Egypt for food but to stay in the land of the Philistines in the city of Gerar.

In Genesis 26:4 God told Isaac that, "I will make thy seed to multiply as the stars of heaven, and will give unto thy seed all these countries; and in thy seed shall all the nations of the earth be blessed."

Verse 5 says that Abraham:

- Obeyed My voice
- Kept My charge
- Kept My commandments
- Kept My statutes
- Kept My laws

The reason God required the same obedience status quo from the next generation was because He did not want the next generation to lower the standards neither be deprived from *the open heavens blessing* of the covenant. In other words, if you want what Abraham had, you do what Abraham did.

Then Isaac sowed in that land, and received in the same year an hundredfold and the Lord blessed him. And the man:

- Waxed great

- Went forward

- Grew until he became very great

Genesis 26:12-13

Verse 14 stays that the Philistines envied him. This was an abnormal prosperity, an unusual increase, and an unbelievable success story!

> *The success of every one man in the hands of God is cardinally measured by your ratio of obedience.*

The grace of God empowers you to walk in obedience without fail which also guarantees fulfillment, contentment and the effectual completion of your purpose on Earth. May God's grace insulate your obedience and educate you in the path of righteousness ordained for you. I pray you hold firm and fast to hearing God's voice and being sensitive to the prompting of His Holy Spirit. May you let your light triumph with faith in God over the passion of humanistic logic. Faith keeps your focus, strengthens your drive and increases your capacities and abilities to fulfill your destiny with flying colors.

> *Big dreamers need big faith.*

Long term visionaries need long lasting consistent faith and belief. The power of one man in God's vision requires solid faith and an amazing growing belief system. Your journey may not

111

begin with mega faith but one step at a time makes room for your faith to grow; one more little faith, one more hope. May you increase in the full persuasion of the absolute ability of God to help you because your faith activates increasing help from the invisible God.

It is disconcerting that our generation, in some cases, does not want to pay the price of absolute obedience to God. It is noteworthy that true faith has no alternative; absolute faith moves God. The word of God produces faith as you study and hear. Faith can increase with your increasing attentiveness to the spoken and the written word of God. Everyone on a mission can increase in faith by maintaining their consistency in the Word. Feed your faith by connecting to the Word. Make the Word of God a network project. God has never lowered the standards for any generation. It is His pleasure to give us His Kingdom and all that He has, including all that He is but *the key is receiving faith from His Word.* It is a mystery to understand that the same God who has awesome blessings for you will also give you the faith to work and walk with Him. This almost sounds like the chairman of a bank giving you the keys to the vault so you can access any money that you want, but he must first indeed give you the keys. God is full of all you need for your journey and His word makes faith available to fuel your accelerations and manifestation. Faith is what we have from God but belief is what we do to fulfill the dreams and purpose deposited into our hearts and put into our hands. Faith does not lower the standard; it maintains it for the high ways of God for your life. The unfortunate scenario of our busy, advanced technological world threatens our investment of faith into the principles of God. Nothing pleases God more than our faith in His word. Dare to please Him by walking the thin line of faith and the narrow path for your journey; His glory shall be with you and in you, as you arrive on the other side with crowns and celebrations of joy. There is always a great story at the end of a journey full of faith.

Obedience to God requires sacrifice.

Absolute obedience requires absolute sacrifice and partial obedience results in partial results. God is an absolute and therefore demands absolute obedience. Many often say, "I have been obeying God and yet not seeing the results." In some cases it's because the time for the results hasn't come, which then requires patience. For by faith and patience the elders obtained the promises (Hebrews 6:11). In other cases, it is as a result of partial sacrifices, which are inadequate to augment your obedience to the full desire of God. It is equivalent to a half tank of fuel in your car for a journey that requires a full tank. We therefore make logical conclusions a law, in the equation of God, and even sometimes label it as a "practical faith." The truth is faith is not practical in terms of logical expectations that coincide with common sense. Faith is a powerful, spiritual law fueled by the Word of an Almighty God who is a Spirit. John 4:24 says that God is a Spirit and they that worship Him, must worship Him in spirit and in truth. Therefore, faith is a spiritual principle employed by believing the omnipotence of God to produce natural results beyond human limitations.

Faith therefore is vertical inspiration producing horizontal results above human levels.

It is also a fruit and a gift of the Holy Spirit, received into your system by meditating on the Word of God. This creates in the natural mind a spiritual system of divine activations and inspirations for performance of the divine kind. A person of faith is one who believes totally in leaning not on his own understanding but in all his way acknowledging God and His reality to change circumstances without eluding the reality of a practical challenge.

The days in which we are seem to suggest instant results for little or no price. This mindset makes room for more comfort and less sacrifice, yet with high expectation of results, much more than the actual investment. This euphoria has weakened the standard for quality resolution needed for results. Some want to see the glory of God without paying any price of giving Him the attention that is needed to enter His presence so as to see His glory. Absolute faith in God provokes His absolute power to your advantage. There is power in one singular person who dares to pay the total price to make the difference he was designed and ordained to make.

CHAPTER 14:

KING DAVID

Born in Bethlehem to his father Jesse, David had seven other brothers with great prominence and promise on each of them. The intriguing story of David as the last born, characterizes the ability of God to choose anyone, according to His own deep counsels, for the singular purpose of fulfilling extraordinary divine plans. The power of one man lies within a true exposition of the sovereign act of God in the life of individuals. Is there anything too hard for God?

David and his story looked like a replacement of King Saul whose disobedience to the instructions of the Lord qualified his disapproval in the sight of God. In God's great disappointment He said that He had regretted ever making Saul king because

Saul dishonored Him.

> *Then came the word of the Lord unto Samuel, saying, it repenteth me that I have set up Saul to be king: for he is turned back from following me, and hath not performed my commandments. And it grieved Samuel; and he cried unto the Lord all night.* **Samuel 15:10-11**

> *And Samuel said, Hath the Lord as great delight in burnt offerings and sacrifices, as in obeying the voice of the Lord? Behold, to obey is better than sacrifice, and to hearken than the fat of rams. For rebellion is as the sin of witchcraft, and stubbornness is as iniquity and idolatry. Because thou hast rejected the word of the Lord, he hath also rejected thee from being king.* **Samuel 15:22-23**

The word rebellion is used to describe the state of Saul's character in the hand of the God of heaven and earth. It is important to indicate here that God always demands absolute obedience to work with Him. In the Garden of Eden before the fall, God had total obedience to work with but from after the fall the reverse became the fact. In Genesis 6:3 the Lord said that His spirit shall not continue to strive with men for their hearts are constantly evil. This means that God honors the choice of man's will even in the atmosphere of His sovereign glory. The call of God, the mandate, the anointing and the supernatural gifts endowed upon a man or a people, are God's decision but the choice to obey is within the scope of man's decision. Every plan of God for the individual does not go beyond the obedience and the will of man.

> ***The extent to which your will is yielded in the hands of Jehovah is the extent to which He advances His counsel in your life.***

In Gethsemane, the last battle of Christ before the crucifixion was of His will; his determination to lay it down in absolute brokenness, before His Father, was the key to His triumph over the enemy and the fulfillment of the call of God upon His life. In the dynamics of *the power of one* in the hands of God, the management of man's will power cannot be ignored. Use your will wisely and never against what you know the mind of God is for you to do or not to do.

Recently, as I drove in my car, I felt the presence of God in the vehicle in what seemed to be a dialogue. I remember the Lord said how intrigued He is when watching how men apply their will. Startled by the word *intrigue*, I was amazed to discern how particularly God watches the gymnastics of man's will even in His presence. There are many who are favored by God, strengthened by God and advanced by God yet will consistently attempt to manipulate God because of His great mercy. For you to excel I pray you deal with the subject of the will.

> *Sacrifice and offering thou didst not desire; mine ears hast thou opened: burnt offering and sin*

offering hast thou not required. Then said I, Lo, I come: in the volume of the book it is written of me, I delight to do thy will, O my God: yea, thy law is within my heart. I have preached righteousness in the great congregation: lo, I have not refrained my lips, O LORD, thou knowest. **Psalms 40:6-9**

Obedience cannot be substituted for sacrifice; however, thorough obedience always requires a thorough sacrifice. May the Lord breathe strength into your will-power and may He inspire within you the joy of laying down your will for the Master's use. A German poet once said "What use am I, if I am not of use to God?" David became an incredible solution to the disappointment Saul brought in God's sight. The Lord said He found one among the sons of Jesse who would do His counsel; a man after His own heart. Every person in the hand of God, in the days of His manifestation, is expected to be a person after God's own heart. What a track record of favor!

In 1 Samuel 16:1, the rejection of Saul was a bitter blow to Samuel; not only because of the pain of seeing a man lose his purpose but also the difficulty of accepting the failure of a king who was anointed by Samuel with integrity. By this I mean that for any time where a man or woman of God lays hands on someone or by the will of God becomes a spiritual father or mother to that person, your integrity goes along with that person. Therefore, in the event of disappointments, there is a reflection on the spiritual leadership under which they function.

The Lord said to Samuel, for how long will mourn for Saul seeing that have rejected him from reigning over Israel? Fill thy horn with oil and go, I will send thee to Jesse the Bethlehemite for I have provided me a king among his sons. **I Samuel 16:1**

In verse 13, Samuel took the horn and anointed David in the midst of his brethren and the Spirit of the Lord came upon David *from that day forward.*

———————— ❦ ————————

CHAPTER 15:

PURPOSE AND TRANSFORMATION

Purpose is the reason why a thing is created; it is also the thoughts and reasoning which proceed the design and functionality of anything needed to advance a vision. It is a gift of God attached to every individual who is released into time by birth. Knowing that God creates everything for a reason; a purpose establishes the relevance of creation. It is an act of self-determination in life, knowing God and His will to fulfill.

Jeremiah 9:23-24 reveals that the greatest thing in God's sight - when it comes to purpose and achievements - is not in what we do but what we know of Him and receive of Him to do. Wise, mighty, and wealthy people often have the tendency of naturally celebrating their achievements and congratulating themselves for what has been accomplished, but in all this we see King Solomon's wisdom:

> *There are many devices in a man's heart; nevertheless the counsel of the Lord that shall stand.*
>
> **Proverbs 19:21 (KJV)**

> *Many plans are in a man's mind, But it is the Lord's purpose for him that will stand (be carried out).*
>
> **Proverbs 19:21 (AMP)**

The separation between devices in our hearts and the purpose of God is very intriguing. The pragmatic slant of every hard working person is to lean towards devices in his heart. Can you imagine how many intriguing ideas we all subject our thinking cycles to daily, weekly and within a lifetime? I am making reference to the several good ideas or devices to manipulate a system or utilize available resources and opportunities as a means to an end; but in all this, God sovereignly ends up blocking our devices which are not in accordance with His God ideas. The battle ground here is divided between good devices and God purposes. Praise God for what you do, but to imagine that it can be considered as devices of men, other then the purpose of God, is thought provoking. It is a wealthy life to live according to God's exact passion. It is what I consider sweeter then honey for contentment, if only we can shift from great devices into God's master plan for our lives.

Adam and Eve were swerved from their God given mandate by the evil one trapping them with a good idea. Satan provoked, "you will have knowledge and understanding." Truth being told, they had the knowledge and understanding already. May we graduate from good to right.

> *By faith Moses, when he was come to years, refused to be called the son of Pharaoh's daughter; choosing rather to suffer affliction with the people of God, than to enjoy the pleasures of sin for a season; esteeming the reproach of Christ greater riches than the treasures in Egypt: for he had respect unto the recompense of the reward. By faith he forsook Egypt, not fearing the wrath of the king for he endured, as seeing him who is invisible.* **Hebrews 11:24-27**

Faith is not given to us to acquire things hoped for, but also so we can refuse the good opportunities in order to preserve the right opportunities of purpose. Accepting good things is a generic attribute of the ordinary man, but having the fortitude to refuse good things and invest into the right thing is an unusual feat which sets apart in every society and generation the good from the great and great from the greatest. Uniqueness is the spine of relevance, but few are they that obtain it. It is encouraging to know that the ability to make a choice between good and right, is an attribute of all man kind, but being able to pay the price for the unique purpose of God requires discipline and tough approaches to simple demands.

By faith Moses refused to be called the son of Pharaoh's daughter. What an incredible statement. Moses was a prince in preparation to become head of the Egyptian government. He was well educated with the learnings of Egypt, which was the birth ground for all civilization at that time. It is believed he attained professorship of humanities in today's standards. He was taught the etiquette, the mannerisms, and the ways of excellence in leadership; trained to be logical and effective, Moses had it made. He had a state of life that anybody in those days would pay any price to have. He was soon to become the celebrated president of the "then" first world, Egypt.

But the scripture says when he came of age, meaning when maturity gripped him, he saw through the compromise of glory versus the unattractive pain of swapping what was at hand with what was afar off, but was the true choice of God for him. Purpose is that one original reason why a person is created before God, but in most cases difficult to identify not having the right keys or tools to work with. The influence of society, culture of existence, pressure of the status quo and wanting to be what you really are not made to be, usually creates a wall that fights decision and revelation of the perfect will of God.

The encouragement here is that what ever came into the heart of Moses to refuse the snare of temporary glory, so as to obtain the package of a future permanent, eternal success story, is available today. Have faith and believe that it is possible to jump off the cliff of the known into the ocean of the unknown believing the invisible hands are with you in mid-air. Moses did so from the Egyptian heights but was caught mid-air by the eternal hands of purpose, which prevented him from crashing in the valley below. Rather he navigated through the skies of favor and destiny to land on the other side of hope and achievement in God's sight. With absolute contentment he had a great gain of success. It is often said, "nothing comes easy." Even if it is an ordained gift of God you need to contribute your decisive preferences and willful choice in response. In other words, every mandate and gift of God needs the words, "yes I do!" or as Mary the mother of Jesus said to angel Gabriel, "Be it unto me according to your words" (Luke 1:37-38).

If Moses by faith rejected the accolade of royal son-ship to Pharaoh's daughter, but chose to connect to the perceived purpose of God for him, it means:

- He exercised his faith to obtain the reason why he was born.
- He used faith to reject the obstructions of purpose.
- Faith gave him the ability to discern right from wrong against all odds.
- By faith he saw beyond the glitziness of the natural opportunity to obtain eternal grandeur of glorious leadership and dominion.
- By faith he obtained a good report before eternity and time, heaven and earth.

This kind of discernment is essential for every one person traversing through this high-tech, logical world and culture. If there is a time we need His help to see through our world's opportunities to obtain the golden mandate of God's pleasure for us, it is now. Isaiah speaks concerning Christ, who was called Immanuel:

> *Butter and honey shall He eat, that He may know*
> *to refuse the evil and choose the good.* **Isaiah 7:15**

The metaphor of honey and butter is very relevant to everyone chosen to run the race of destiny. Synonymous to enlightenment and illumination, *understanding* is cardinal for the pathways mapped out by the infinite God for the finite man. It boosts your personal conviction as to what you are called for. It establishes your drive for a cause and an insatiable hunger for achievement. Illumination produced by butter and honey makes you unstoppable. It makes you master of your decisions. You have to know. You have to understand. You have to discern. Honey brings illumination prophetically and butter, which is the product of the churning of milk, gives insightfulness through the process of your mandate. This makes you wiser and deeper than surface values. May we obtain our butter and honey as we refuse brass to obtain gold; every generation needs it. Desire therefore the gifting of the Holy Spirit, for your understanding to be made whole.

In Isaiah 11:3 Christ is known to have quick understanding so as not to judge after the sight of the eyes nor by the hearing of the ear. Every logical being is influenced by sight and sound predominantly. It is therefore a proven fact that the more your eyes and ears repeatedly connect to an environment, the sooner it becomes part of you. Your judgment and decisions, are plateaued thereby. Having said this, just as the law of gravity is defeated by aerodynamics, the gift of understanding breaks you away from the status quo and the averaging of life's natural influences. We were created to rule and have dominion and determine outcomes and not for outcomes to determine us. We make things happen, it's who we are, but it takes the sharp sensitivity of a true leader to navigate through invisible walls that appear real.

In I Kings 3:8 King Solomon asked the Lord for an understanding heart to judge the people that he may discern good and bad. This request pleased the Lord God so greatly that He gave Solomon more then he desired. Verse 12-14. He gave him what he asked for and added riches, honor and wisdom, far much more than all thing kings before him and after him. Great movers and shakers of every generation are required to walk by exclusive understandings so they can maneuver through visible and invisible obstacles, within the time frame given to them to fulfill their mandates. Every singular person on this journey of fulfillment needs an understanding heart. Moses had it, David had it, Solomon, Paul, Christ and all the admired success stories we know, needed it. It's your turn now.

Prophet Isaiah, who had already been a prophet for the first five chapters, suddenly encountered His Creator and saw how far away He was from God's original plan (Isaiah 6:1, 5-8). Even though being celebrated as the king's "palace prophet" was going well for him, Isaiah comes to a sudden rude shock of how he had been influenced by ungodly lips and the conversational lingo of his days. In this rude awakening from a good life and the need for the right one, he felt helpless, not knowing what to do. Suddenly the goodness of God caused an angel to intervene by placing a coal of fire to his lips and removing the iniquity that separated him from the true purpose of God. This being done to him, Isaiah was pulled back in to the highway of purpose ordained for him. There are many on this planet who need to be pulled back into this high frequency of God's purpose driven inspiration; a platform of the highest level of favor, relevance, fulfillment and dominion. Take charge of your life with the discipline of humility to say, "I was wrong."

As a baby willfully throws open its arms to the father's uplift, throw your arms up into the sky of hope and believe in the resurrection power of God to restore you even now. May this restoration heal your mind, your will and your emotions. May it regenerate your spirit and tune your flesh aright. May your life be that symphony and melody that makes God's heart tick. I pray this day that you become the fragrance of your generation in which you were born. May you attract others back to the love life and love lace of God through obedience.

May this be your time today that whatsoever ensnared you from that perfect highway of your mandate, be removed. As the scales fall off your eyes, refuse the culture of compromise and lay hold of the highway of excellence!

In Isaiah 6:8 he hears the word of the Lord saying, "Whom shall I send and who will go for us?" This is one of the most intriguing scripture verses in the Old Testament revealing an aspect of the nature of God not to impose His plans upon you, but rather inspire you in the right way with love and firmness of assurance. "Whom shall I send" in a present singular tense, in this case the Triune God: the Father, the Son and the Holy Spirit, speaking to a man they created on the earth for an assignment; but backing it up as one voice. The Lord God said, "Who shall go for us?" In other words, the Godhead created the prophet in unity of purpose hoping to derive personal and individual contentment and joy from the singular achievement and obedience of Isaiah. This suggestively says that on the day you receive your final rewards in heaven, you get to be celebrated by the Father, the Son and the Holy Ghost and all the individual achievers of heaven that day, being called by the one God yet celebrated by the Triune God. It also reveals the true hope of our calling which to God has far much more contentment and joy, to see us fulfill His will, more than anything else we can ever offer Him. Isaiah responded, "Send me, here am I." The call and the mandate comes from the Lord, but the response (not a reaction) is our honorable responsibility.

May your life be an asset to the glory of God!

In Philippians 3:7-15 Paul takes the same stand as Moses, Isaiah and the many who took part in God's *role call of honor* by letting go what seemed favorable and laying hold with joy to what pleased God: purpose. Apostle Paul said, "That I might attain the resurrection of the dead and being able to apprehend the purpose for which I was apprehended, I'm forgetting those things which are behind and reaching forth for the things before me, pressing hard towards the mark of the high calling."

Purpose separates you from self-gratification to a higher level of gratification. Contentment and value are downloaded into your spirit by the Lord. For us, it is the perfect will of God in eternity, downloaded into a yielded spirit of individuals for fulfillment. This amazing mandate is an extraordinary gift of God that turns a person around effectively. When God's plan is accepted, the grace to implement it is released without fail. This makes you very relevant to God causing you to obtain favor with God and man. It increases your stature and effectiveness before time and eternity. As in Luke 2:52 Jesus increased in wisdom and stature and favor with God and man, being obedient to the purpose of the Father. The dimension of joy and fulfillment which comes along with this principle makes authors mad. It is the kind of love experience that beats reasoning. Obedience toward the purpose of God connects you to unlimited joy regardless the price and the pain. As much as the nine months of pregnancy is uncomfortable for a woman, talking up the pain of child birth makes it worse. In the end, the safe delivery of a living baby outweighs it all. The unbelievable sense of contentment and satisfaction beyond words seems to reverberate into the very being of every mother. Whereas it is called delivery (being delivered of a burden) the celebration which comes from pain is a lifetime admiration and the pride of contributing life into a generation's process of fulfillment and productivity. Carry your pregnancy of purpose according to the will of God wisely.

In Paul's encouragement to his spiritual son, or leadership intern Timothy, he presents solid words of hope and bravery:

- I have fought the good fight
- I have finished my cause
- I have kept the faith

I think in agreement with Paul, there are good reasons to fight for your purpose, but much more so to finish the demands of purpose by keeping the principles that are required for attainment. Paul's message here gives a picture of an American football game, or a soccer game or a basketball game; conclusively the player with the ball draws the most attack. So also, Paul tells Timothy not to underestimate the demands of purpose on a person or vision. You will face contentions, controversies and contrary winds because purpose always makes you walk against the tide. Consistent and to be expected is the tidal wave that attacks vision and great dreams. As in sports, when the ball of purpose is with you, the focus of attackers are drawn to your direction. It takes a determined person to fight a good fight within the rules that you might attain the prize for achievements. Paul instills an incredible passion in this young man by saying that it is OK to keep your eye on the crown, the final day.

> *I have fought a good fight, I have finished my course,*
> *I have kept the faith. Henceforth there is laid up*
> *for me a crown of righteousness, which the Lord,*
> *the righteous judge, shall give me at that day: and*

*not to me only, but unto all them also that love his
appearing.* **II Timothy 4:7-8**

I think Jesus was able to go through the pain of the cross, knowing for a fact that there was an incredible glory that awaited Him, if only He could endure the pain. Truly far beyond the joy of the crown of glory and honor in heaven, is the eternal, unequivocal truth that you made God happy by fulfilling His heart's desire about you. I think it would be a wonderful thing for God to set His eye on you with a nod and the biggest smile to say, "you please me well."

Aghh! There is nothing greater than that.

These are the kinds of inspirations that motivated Esther (Esther 4:15-16) and the three Hebrew boys (Daniel 3:16-18). Esther said, "I will go for it, even if I perish". The three Hebrew boys echoed the same inspiration in their days by declaring to King Nebuchadnezzar that they would not bow to his god even if they burned. They believed their God would deliver them declaring, "even if He doesn't, we shall not bow and we shall not burn, by faith. There is something about the provocation of exclusive faith, courage and a master minded focus that sets the individual apart to face their calling in the midst of colossal negativity and doubt. It's almost like saying eternity turns on the fire of God within you, which you never knew you had. As if God presses a single button in heaven, that turns on your purpose, and turns off the world inside of you; programming you for glory.

Thus David the son of Jesse reigned over all Israel.

And the time that he reigned over Israel was forty years; seven years reigned he in Hebron, and thirty and three years reigned he in Jerusalem.

1 Chronicles 29:26-27

Verse 28 says that David died:

- In a good old age
- Full of days
- Full of riches
- Full of honor

A purpose driven life therefore is the God mandated life for a person worth living. May this be your story at the bright end of the long tunnel of purpose.

Question: How do you identify purpose from the devices (carnal schemes) of a human heart?

Answer:

a) Accept purpose as a gift of God.

b) It is that vision that is doomed to fail unless by the dominant help of God.

c) The inborn peace, contentment, and a sense of great fulfillment that comes along with it.

d) It is that mandate that arrests your attention and your spirit with a God feeling

e) It is that which your spirit and God's spirit connect to with doubtless agreement.

Apprehending the purpose of God stirs up the jealousy of God over your life with such passion. It is that consistent feeling of God chasing after you wherever you go and whatever you do; drawing your attention to what His glorious will for you is. It is usually a battle God never loses. I will say a righteous man is ordained by God to win every battle of adversity, but programed to lose the battle against God. In losing the battle of your will against God's will, you attain the highest order of life, existence, and blessings.

THE POWER OF DECLARATION AND CONVICTION

It is an amazing insight to see how dear God's purpose is to His personal being, delight and nature. Of purpose, the scripture says, He makes solid declarations in ancient past into the unknown future to create the vision in accomplishment before it is revealed. Isaiah 46:10 talks about declaring the end from the beginning, which means we are to fulfill and accomplish the work of God when we are called. This is to say, He finishes the work in its beauty and entirety for glory before we even start the physical journey of destiny. If this is so then our obedience to His instruction is paramount. His inspirations guide us into the ordained steps that bring us to the desired goal which is always glorious. Since the end is always better than the beginning according to scripture, then the end result of every person who dares to step into the unique call shall see great accomplishments.

Proverbs 4:18 says the path of the righteous gets brighter and brighter unto the end. If there are any pitfalls on the way, based on our frailties and human weaknesses, the power of God's love turns them around for our good, because ultimately His purpose shall stand. Romans 8:28-30 declares that all things work together for our good, according to His purpose. This means the mandate of God for His purpose will not fail. It is the reason why God attaches great love to those who dare to partner with Him. For His accomplishments to stand as He decided, God would have to give great grace to as many as are called by love. In His love we find the elasticity of His grace, the flexibility of the anointing and the all time power of productivity through His word.

Deuteronomy 23:5 reveals that God, for His love sake, turns curses into blessings. If God's purpose is so dear to Him then as many as connect to His purpose will be dear to Him too. If some of the errors you have made have not been turned around yet, may God turn the back-log of troubles around for you speedily according to His purpose! Keep trusting, believing and confessing His goodness and you shall eat the fruit of your lips. It is time for misfortunes to be turned into blessings! Just as John the Baptist made the crooked paths straight for Christ, so are we to walk this mandated journey with straight ways, without excessive gorges, dangerous turns and rugged peak mountains. The bulldozer that levels the mountains and rugged roads, is the word of God. Speak the word and keep pushing forward! If He can declare the end from the beginning, you can do so as well, declaring your success and all tough times into fulfillment with hope. For Joshua, God spoke to him saying this book of the law shall not depart from you.

> *This book of the law shall not depart out of thy mouth; but thou shalt meditate therein day and night, that thou mayest observe to do according to all that is written therein: for then thou shalt make thy way prosperous, and then thou shalt have good success.* **Joshua 1:8**

Meditation on the Word keeps your mind clear and pure. It keeps the vision sanctified and your soul focused. The word enlightens your path and keeps you faith-fitted. In Jeremiah 1:9-10 the Lord touched Jeremiah's lips and said, I have put my words in thy mouth. Through the dynamics of the Living Word, Jeremiah had power of kingdoms to root out, pull down, to destroy, to throw down, to build and to plant. The pathway of purpose as divine as it is, for every individual, requires the application of the Kingdom principles of determination, passion and continuity in faith. You have to *make it happen* as you are being guided through the principles of obedience.

In Genesis 1:3, God said, "Let there be light and there was light." In this context because God SAID specifically what He wanted, he SAW exactly what He desired. What you want to SEE is what you must SAY.

If you don't want to see it, then don't say it.

Declare in your meditations, contemplations and activities,

what needs to be seen. Keep saying it. Keep believing it. Keep confessing it. It is the secret to creativity and immeasurable success. Your declarations create your world and relate to your singular journey. As it is said, carnal words produce carnal results; spiritual words produce spiritual results; fruitful words produce fruitful results; lastly, God-words confessed produce God-results.

The scripture cannot be broken.

This is good news to every singular person on the journey of purpose, destiny and leadership. If the scriptures are available to everybody, rich or poor then we all have the same plain field to start with. It starts right from believing what God says in His word concerning you. Meditation on the Word of God feeds your spirit, mind, will and emotions with light and staying power. It keeps your mental systems healthy, clean, and alive. The incubation of the Word of God also produces faith, which the Bible says comes by hearing and hearing by the Word of God. If this statement is true then there are certain things that you hear that produce the opposite of faith which include fear, doubt, anxiety and the consistency of instability. Faith and purpose drive your journey into destiny. Every purpose needs an investment of faith to succeed. Since God is the giver of purpose, it is expedient that we believe that He exists and is a rewarder of those who diligently seek Him for who He is. The directions He has and the help He offers is for our prosperity. He told Joshua to meditate on the Word day and night so that he will have good success. The subject of good success is the perfection of purpose for Joshua.

Without faith it is impossible to please God which means the way to please God is blocked without the key of faith. Faith is an incredible delicacy of God that attracts His attention. It gives Him the legal atmosphere to perfect His counsel in the atmosphere of the earth.

If the Lord shall visit your home, shall he find faith? What if He comes into your heart, your business, your office, shall He find faith? What if He takes a peep into your mind, shall He find faith? He truly is not looking for equipped or educated people; neither is He looking for those who are properly ready, but rather those who are available with a desire to believe. You need to invest, deliberately, faith into Jesus' name. Have faith that God is bigger than you and believe that He is who He says He is and therefore is willing and able to fulfill all His promises in partnership with your availability and desires. The greatest network on this earth is networking with God and His world of glory.

SET AND SUBSET

The subject of purpose can't be adequately explained without signifying the truth that all purpose, in heaven and earth, are established in Christ. This is to say, outside the firstborn Son of God, the most anointed in heaven and the earth, there is no desire of God, nor purpose to be achieved.

For he whom God hath sent speaketh the words of

God: for God giveth not the Spirit by measure unto him. The Father loveth the Son, and hath given all things into his hand.   **John 3:34-36**

The Father gave Christ His spirit without measure as well as putting all things into His hands. It is therefore valid to say that when you miss Jesus the Son of God, you have missed eternity and its blissful promise of hope and fulfillment. There is nothing else God has for you outside of Christ.

According to the eternal purpose which he purposed in Christ Jesus our Lord in whom we have boldness and access with confidence by the faith of him.

Ephesians 3:11-12

Paul establishes this incredible revelation and truth to the church of Ephesus that every eternal purpose is loaded in the purpose of Christ. For that matter, the very existence of Christ our Lord and Savior, and all that He is in itself the manifest proof of God's purpose forever. It is an incredible joy to note that in our search to knowing purpose, all the options have been deleted and simplified in one purpose. For me this is an incredible blessing, knowing the danger in missing the mark, if we were to go look for purpose on our own, in the created world in which we are. I thank God for making it simple through His kindness that we can attain purpose through relationship with Christ. This is a true blessing.

If this is so, then Hebrews 1:2-3 is valid, which says God

speaks through His son, by whom all things were made, being the brightness of God's glory.

> *God, who at sundry times and in divers manners spake in time past unto the fathers by the prophets, hath in these last days spoken unto us by his Son, whom he hath appointed heir of all things, by whom also he made the worlds; Who being the brightness of his glory, and the express image of his person, and upholding all things by the word of his power, when he had by himself purged our sins, sat down on the right hand of the Majesty on high:*

Hebrews 1:2-3

By these three scripture patterns we can emphatically say, Christ is the complete set of God's purpose in time and eternity. Every other purpose of men, nations, people, generations and creation, are derived out of Christ. This means if Christ is the "complete set," then our individual purpose (as *the power of one)* is the "subset" of Christ's purpose.

As in Colossians 1:18 Christ is:

- The head
- The beginning
- The first born
- That in all things He might have the pre-eminence.

Being pre-eminent simply means that He is the consistency of all matter and the flourishing existence of the visible and the invisible world. This proof alludes to the fact that the absence of the dominion of Jesus is the presence of vacuum. So long as there is no vacuum in creation and in heaven, Christ is the relevance of time and eternity. So when I have Christ, I am in the right place to fulfill purpose. It means also that I have all it takes to achieve the word, the will and the ways of God.

Colossians 1:8-9 says, "For it pleased the Father that in Him all fullness should dwell." This scripture explains why life truly begins when we meet Jesus and augments His cardinal saying that, without Me you can do nothing (John 15:5). The people of Colossae in the days of Apostle Paul, received an inspired eye opener from Paul's epistles. Establishing this one truth in Colossians 2:9-10 that for in Him dwells all the fullness of the Godhead bodily, for which cause we are complete in Him. I dare to say that based on these scriptures that it is a dangerous proposition to postpone or suspend your life from yielding to Christ. It simply alludes to the fact that delaying your encounter with Christ is putting your purpose on a pending file, willfully or ignorantly. He is truly the way the truth and the life (John 14:6). I found purpose when I yielded my life to Jesus. I lost nothing but the devil and gained all that God is and has for me. Connecting to Christ is the joy of inheriting God and embracing son-ship in Him to the intent that we have become heirs of God and joint heirs with Christ Jesus. So purpose is not only achieving relevance in society, but also having a state of being in Christ; that also is purpose. It is a valid equation to believe that to be fulfilled in your purpose is to be in the state of purpose called, having the divine nature.

So if I have Christ, I have God's purpose. If Christ be in me, then I can do nothing but fulfill His purpose. It means, fulfilling purpose, is fulfilling Christ and fulfilling Christ is fulfilling God's purpose. I am done (fulfilled) in God by having Christ in me the true hope of glory. I say, as Christ is the complete set of God's purpose, I am a subset of God's purpose in Christ.

TIMING AND FULFILLMENT

In the script of King Solomon, one of the wisest kings that ever lived in the Old Testament, he states that there is a season for everything under the heavens and a time for every purpose (Ecclesiastes 3:11). His revelation of purpose and time, working together, is outstanding. He is saying, that for time to be well spent, purpose must be fulfilled, and without purpose time is irrelevant. This also means that anyone who purposefully utilizes their time on earth becomes essential to their generation. Mankind was made to produce results according to the original plan of God. As in Genesis 1:28, God blessed them and said:

- Be fruitful
- Multiply
- Replenish
- Subdue
- Have dominion

This five-fold blessing released by God on man, DNA's God's purpose. Anything that is purposed in God is designed to produce the composite package of these five dynamics of blessing. The greatest tragedy on earth is not a fatal car accident, a plane crash or an earthquake, etc., but it is to leave this earth without fulfilling the reason you were created.

Purpose should be every humans highest focus. There are many plans that run through our minds and hearts daily, which do not necessarily address the pivot of purpose. Purpose is that which God predestined you to be; it is wise-heartedness to search it out, find it and pursue it. Proverbs 19:21 says, "There are many devices in a man's heart, but the purpose of God alone shall stand." If that is true, which it is, it means for every one thousand thoughts which may go through a man's mind, it's likely just one percent - or even none - is connected to the true and perfect will of God. There is more vanity on this earthy than purpose.

The discovery and manifestation of purpose is cardinal in the heart of God, because it absolutely defines His reasoning concerning you and everything He does. Consequently heaven protects every purpose by counsel; which means there is only one way to establish God's purpose on the earth, through the revelation of His deep counsel. Proverbs 15:22 says that, without counsel purpose is defeated. Proverbs 20:18 says that, every purpose is established by counsel.

The Spirit of counsel is the very deep wisdom of heaven, which comes by inspiration, upon chosen vessels called of God for unique assignments. This great power of divine counsel has such great grace and direction to the extent that it changes the life pattern of everybody that receives the call to purpose. It is transformational! It is a mystery to see the lifestyle of people or an individual who apprehends the reason they were born and a wonderful thing to behold when the Mighty God of all creation, the only wise God, apprehends a person. So much more beautiful is the story when that person yields their life to apprehend the reason for which they were apprehended. It is the one singular exploit every person on this earth should behold. It is the glory of God to conceal the matter of purpose, but the honor of kings to search it out and find it (Proverbs 25:2).

- Oh if I can find my purpose, I will walk in my high places!
- If I can find my purpose, I can run and not be weary, I can walk and not faint!
- I will mount up with wings as eagles.
- I will fear not the snare of the fowler.
- I will run through troops and leap over walls.
- If I can find my purpose I will look beyond pain and lay hold of the joy that awaits me on the other side!

I will certainly meet you all on the top!

Purpose is like a positive steroid to people of destiny. God finds nobodies and puts upon them the governing power of purpose and the end result is always good news; it is the biggest transformation creation has ever known. So goes the saying that a man who is born of the Spirit is like the wind. Jesus explains to Nicodemus in their dialogue about why a man should be born again; it's all about purpose! There is always a moment in time for every one person who finds favor in the sight of the Lord for destiny; a time when purpose meets with grace in a kairos moment. This kind of encounter always seems to draw a fine line between the past of your life and the beginning of an unprecedented journey with God into the unknown; *from that day forward!*

John records the meeting between Christ and Nicodemus in a divine time frame allotted to guide Nicodemus into his purpose:

> *There was a man of the Pharisees, named Nicodemus, a ruler of the Jews: The same came to Jesus by night, and said unto him, Rabbi, we know that thou art a teacher come from God: for no man can do these miracles that thou doest, except God be with him. Jesus answered and said unto him, Verily, verily, I say unto thee, Except a man be born again, he cannot see the kingdom of God. Nicodemus saith unto him, How can a man be born when he is old? Can he enter the second time into his mother's womb, and be born? Jesus answered, Verily, verily, I say unto thee, Except a man be born of water and of the Spirit, he cannot enter into the Kingdom of God. That which is born of the flesh is flesh; and that which is born of the Spirit is spirit. Marvel not*

that I said unto thee, Ye must be born again. The wind bloweth where it listeth, and thou hearest the sound thereof, but canst not tell whence it cometh, and whither it goeth: so is every one that is born of the Spirit.　　　　　　　**John 3:1-8**

This encounter is relevant for every person created to fulfill an ultimate call for God. For instance, Nicodemus was one of only two people honored to handle the dead body of Jesus after His death. Christ's body was prepared for burial by the privileged Nicodemus and Joseph of Arimathea (John 19:38-42).

The encounter with a divine personality like Christ, is the reason why Nicodemus found his purpose. This means the decision was made in heaven before the foundation of the world, concerning His purpose to bring perfect conclusion to the physical life and ministry of Christ upon the earth. Until Nicodemus got born again and connected to the right vein of relationship with God through Christ, that purpose would have remained unaccomplished. The counsel of God was the introduction of salvation or being *born again* to Nicodemus. It is prudent to say that every purpose needs a specific counsel to advance its course and manifest the specific reason why it was put on earth. From that day forward Nicodemus found his place in the divine agenda, which made him relevant in his generation.

In every one individual there is always a drawing line, which creates a demarcation in time, bringing separation of seasons from one to the next. This demarcation of time has always clearly shown the difference between the past and the future, the old and the new, the previous and the now; the old wineskin and the new wineskin; in the life of Christ it is the B.C. and the A.D.

- For Noah it was when they entered the ark before the flood.
- For Abraham it was when God called him out of Meso-potamia.
- For Joseph it was when he was brought out of prison and into the palace.
- For Gideon it was when he was encountered by the angel of the Lord
- For Esther it was when she said, before the three day fast, "If I perish I perish."
- For the disciples it was on the day of Pentecost, when the Holy Ghost came upon them as a rushing mighty wind.
- For Saul who became Paul it was the Damascus road encounter with the resurrected Christ.
- For all saints, generically it is the day of your salvation, the transformation from a sinner to a saint; specifically it is the day you apprehend your call and purpose for an intimate walk with the Holy Spirit.

It is usually a kind of shift that can never be forgotten so long as one lives. You will always remember when the divine encountered you to change your course of direction, views and perception; *from that day forward*. It is very transformational and impacts your spirit, soul and body. This kind of osmosis can literally make you into a new creation; where old things pass away and all things become new. This inspiration of the divine kind comes upon you as an anointing that causes you to perform far above your natural limits for every duty that lies ahead of you.

The 17 year-old shepherd boy, David encountered a lion and a bear, and single handedly, as one man, prevailed over them in the defense of his father's sheep. In the day of the battle in the Valley of Elah, where Goliath had held the army of Israel spellbound for 40 days, the young king - by the anointing on his life - defeated the Philistine giant in a great victory. This feat earned him a song from the women of Israel, "Saul has killed his thousand and David his ten-thousand." What a blessing to walk in the calling of the "one man grace" to bring liberty and freedom to a nation, impacting generations to come. This is the power of one man walking in the anointing of the Most High God to fulfill purpose.

The truth revealed is seen in your own personal life as you testify how much change you've experienced ever since purpose arrested you. No telling how exciting the records of heaven will look in the life of every one man designated for humongous success stories. Evidently, the focus is not in what you have achieved, but what God has done through you in spite of yourself and your weaknesses. May the power of heaven find you relevant by making you a vessel of mercy, tuned for exploits by the inspiration of El Elyon, the Most High God! In the encounter of Abraham and Melchizedek, the latter made an incredible pronouncement on the former:

> *And Melchizedek king of Salem brought forth bread and wine: and he was the priest of the Most High God. And he blessed him, and said, Blessed be Abram of the Most High God, possessor of heaven and earth: And blessed be the Most High God, which hath delivered thine enemies into thy hand. And he gave him tithes of all. And the king of Sodom said unto Abram, Give me the persons, and take the goods to thyself. And Abram said to the king of Sodom, I have lift up mine hand unto the Lord, the most high God, the possessor of heaven and earth, That I will not take from a thread even to a shoelatchet, and that I will not take any thing that is thine, lest thou shouldest say, I have made Abram rich:* **Genesis 14:18-23**

The mystery of transformation was so rapid in Abraham's life (then Abram) that with so much confidence he rejected the compromising proposal of the King of Sodom and said, "I will not even take a shoelace from you, lest you will say, you have made Abram rich." It is almost as a little child will lift up his hands in yielded confidence that his father or mother will lift them up and carry them on their shoulders. Abraham depicted such a persuaded confidence in finding his purpose in God. He did not come down and lower himself by expecting a man to be his source of supply and provision. What a transformation! He said in many words:

- I am done with average thinking now that I have found my purpose!
- I am done with logical pedigree seeking and accolade!
- Now that I am interlocked in the network of the Most High God, I have found my niche.
- I have found my place.
- I have laid hold on my destiny.
- The baton of the relay race of purpose is now in my hands!
- I will walk on the high ways of God to the ultimate accomplishment of His dreams for my life and my joy for His call.
- I will stay connected to God's sphere of influence and bask in the glory of His presence, performance and activity through the pathway of humility and strength.
- I will run the race with patience and let eternity define my excellence!

CHAPTER 16:

THE SCHOOL OF PURPOSE

A school can be defined as an institution where instruction is given. It is therefore the activity or process of learning under instructors. You personal journey into destiny and leadership is to take you right into eternity. A pathway designed for each person by the Most High God sovereignly. It is usually not the determination of the created but of the Creator. Purpose from God is to be driven on God's highway at an elevation far higher than ours.

Isaiah 56:8-12 says, "The thoughts, the ways, the deeds and the words of the Lord, are far much more higher than ours." Every purpose from God is packaged in these four chemistries. The chemistry of His thoughts, His ways, His deeds and His words frame the standard of His purpose for you. Anything that falls below these standards disintegrate within the devices of men. In other words, a device of man is that which tries to handle God's projects man's way; making it malleable in the hands of mortals.

The immortal God is defined in His immortal ways, thoughts, deeds and words. That said, it is therefore a pathway of endless brightness and leadership skills; a demography which requires strategic tutorship and schooling from the Lord. Scripture being true, "The sons of God are led by the Spirit of God," (Romans 8:14).

The School of Purpose is thereby defined in John 14:26.

> *But the Comforter, which is the Holy Ghost, whom the Father will send in My name, shall teach you all things and will bring to your remembrance whatsoever I said to you.* **John 14:26**

A true purpose from God is doomed to fail in the hands of spiritually illiterate mortal beings that choose their own pathways based on their *literate revelation* of human logic and definitions, not having what it takes to cut through the logic into God's world of revelation, illumination and brightness. For those who dare to walk with Him, the high pathway of God is an endless brightness of awesome skill sets given to you by the Lord through His Holy Spirit and His nine gifts operating to their fullest capacity in your life.

I Corinthians 12:4-7 refers to:

- The diversities of gifts

- Differences of administrations
- Diversities of operations

> *Now there are diversities of gifts, but the same Spirit.*
> *And there are differences of administrations, but the*
> *same Lord. And there are diversities of operations,*
> *but it is the same God, which worketh all in all. But*
> *the manifestation of the Spirit is given to every man*
> *to profit withal.* **I Corinthians 12:4-7**

These three bullet points give us insightfulness of the management brain power of God the Father, the Son and the Holy Spirit. Diversities of gifts, differences of administrations and diversities of operations announce to every student of God the endless multitudes of Kingdom syllabus and wise curriculum that is needed to touch, receive and fulfill ones purpose in the sight of God. Accepting the purpose of God is to enroll in His school for a lifetime. It is the educational process of God's unapproachable light that comes to dwell within us so that we can be standards of expression, direction, edification and comfort to our generation in the times beyond ours.

CHAPTER 17:

THE ENLIGHTENED PATHWAY

Psalm 36:9 says in His light we have light. The incredible participation in the light of the Lord is an inclusion in the covering of the Lord and partnership with His glory. It is an atmosphere of consistent vision, illumination, understanding, alertness, sharpness, soundness of mind, faith, possibility, thinking and creativity. Light is the key to leadership because he who has light, guides the way. In His light we are partakers of the divine nature and influencers of the influenced. It is also an establishment of the chosen vessel in God's domain. You are therefore in the sphere of consistent "mega" fruitfulness. Walking in His light is the key to dominion. You become a steward of all things possessed by God and evidently a multi-blessed personality-walking in His light. A true leader who walks in God's light, feeds on God's light. You were born to feed on His light. The truth is you become what you eat and feeding on God's light makes you see and live and move and abide in the same. The entrance of His word giveth light and it is the desire of God that we walk through the pathways of His greater light which shines to the defeat of darkness. It is not enough to produce leaders of light.

Isaiah 60:1-3 declares, "Arise shine, for thy light is come and the glory of the Lord is risen upon you." Apprehending your purpose is connecting to your pathway of light. Your purpose in God is the enlightened pathway for you. Your light has come because you have connected to God's original purpose. His glory is connected to His purpose for your life. Lay hold on your purpose and you shall be satisfied with the glory of God. Satisfaction is found in walking in the pathway of His perfect will galvanized by His glory.

The absolute light of God with which you have been incubated is the attraction which draws kings and their kingdoms (Isaiah 60:3-7). For God to raise you in His light is for Him to exhibit the beauty that He is for the nations to hunger after him. A humble man of purpose is a lighthouse in God's strategy of Kingdom building. Every person in the hand of God is like a house that contains His light. You are therefore a tower as a lighthouse that draws many out of darkness into the prominence of divine excellence. You attract souls to the heart of God. Shine so all would see the goodness of God. Love His light and you shall be His delight. The consistent meditation of the word of God is the feeding of His light. Feed on His light and you shall be endless light. I invite you into the journey of destiny in leadership through the highway of God's light from time to eternity. Heaven is the final destination of all who love His light. It is the most glorious planet you can dream of. It is a planet of God's lighthouse. Get going thou leader! Find your place!

Receive your calling, for He whom God foreknows, God calls and justifies by His grace to walk on this pristine pathway where we all receive our glorification. Don't resist your calling in God but receive it with gladness for in His light you have light, and nothing will be too hard for you. Light is the source of everything you need to be an achiever, role model and a shining star in the world of God's excellence. True leaders are in a constant fellowship with God's light. This is the person of Jesus, the Light of life. May we raise diligently all those whom we lead, to look like light. May everybody you touch look like Jesus, the ultimate light that changes the world. Light is sown for the righteous. Jesus is the seed of light that was sown by His Father so that He can harvest endless multitudes of enlightened people.

The glory of God produces the pathway of light which we connect to by accepting His purpose above our devices. Psalm 97:11 declares that light is sown for the righteousness and gladness for the upright in heart. There are two major seeds sown by eternity in the pathway of every single person that dares to die to himself or herself to be alive in the Spirit. The first is the seed of light and of gladness. Light is sown for the righteous and gladness is sown for the upright in heart. This is the doing of the Lord and it is marvelous in our sight. The stone, which the builders reject, becomes the cornerstone through the pathway of light. Your love for God's purpose is your love for His light. Your purpose is rooted in God's light and as His countenance shines upon you, his Glory is addictive. Jesus said, Father, glorify Your Son that your Son may glorify Thee. His Son is a seed of light sown by God upon the platform of His incredible purpose. A son becomes the beloved when he forsakes his own way to follows his father's dream. Stay tuned to the glory of God by staying tuned to His purpose and delight for you. Every shining star in God's heart is a fruit of His light. Keep your heart filled with the gladness of light. Rejoice again I say rejoice in the glory that is set before you. For in His light we have light and in His countenance we have victory; but in His glory we abide. Greater love than this, can no man experience, then being established in the light of God. You are a high-breed specimen of a human being when you discover your light through the light of Christ. In His light we have life. This is the light that shines and darkness is demystified (John 1:5). Jesus said he that follows me shall have the light of life and shall not walk in darkness. The roots of unfruitful works of darkness burn instantly when you are sown in light. Negativity loses its character and its place when the righteous receive that light which is sown by His Creator. Every single visionary called by God for this journey is a lover of light, and therefore needs the light of life. Christ is our purpose and the author of our faith. If Christ is the way, the truth and the life, then He is Light that is truth; the Light of that way and the Light of that life. You are therefore a multi enlightened personality when you receive the light of the world as your highway to destiny.

Proverbs 4:18 declares that the pathway of the righteous shines brighter and brighter until the day your purpose is accomplished. To this effect the brightness of our pathways were made so, before our beginning. This is to say every call and purpose of God for one person was determined and virtually choreographed before the foundation of the world. You are therefore designed for that which has already been decided. Bright pathways with all opportunities graphically line up unto perfection for the expected goal, which existed in God's heart before you were born. You were therefore created and designed because of that purpose and that journey. In other words, the goal being set with all expectations and results needed, provoked your creation and the hope of your calling.

CHAPTER 18:

THE CHOREOGRAPHY
OF PURPOSE

Choreography can be defined as the arrangement and the manipulation of actions, which lead to an event. It is also the planning arrangement of steps and patterns of dancers. The Lord orders our steps according to the planned pattern for each and everybody's life based on how He wants you to perform on His stage of purpose. Choose to dance according to the discipline of eternal excellence. We are connected to the pathway of light that shines brighter and brighter as we advance in our journey of destiny.

In the Greek is "khorea" means dance and "graphein" means to write; implying therefore that our purpose is to dance according to what is written. For that matter, God knows exactly what

He has called you for, based on what He has written for you in His book. Christ is the author and the finisher of our faith. Believing in what God says about you is accepting what has been choreographed and written in excellence. You are what God says you are and you will become what He has spoken concerning your life. Purpose is what has been put forth and designed for you. It is also God's smart way of putting you in the right place on eternal map. It's one thing being put on the world map, but its higher fulfillment to be established in God's eternal map as a relevant joy of productivity and beauty. You are wonderfully and fearfully made.

Ecclesiastes says whatsoever God does is perfect and flawless where nothing can be added or taken away from it so those who walk the journey of destiny laid out for them would revere their mandate.

I know that, whatsoever God doeth, it shall be for ever: nothing can be put to it, nor any thing taken from it and God doeth it, that men should fear before him.

- That which hath been is now
- That which is to be hath already been
- And God requireth that which is past

Ecclesiastes 3:14-15

These three stages explain the choreographed purpose by God. Whatever your calling is today, it already existed in God's master plan and mind and that which you are suppose to fulfill in the earth has already been determined, if you walk in obedi-

162

ence. At the end of your journey, God is going to require from you what He expected to gain out of your walk on the earth, for the assignment placed on your shoulders. This almost sounds like God counted the chickens before the eggs were hatched. The choreography of purpose is the definite pathway of one man empowered to cause God's will to be done on earth as it is in heaven. I dare to say that the excellent God is very organized and that which He intends to do on the earth, has already been done in heaven as prototype; therefore its fulfillment can be excellent, having been properly planned and anointed. Revelation 13 says that the Lamb of God was slain before the foundation of the world *in eternity*, before He was crucified on Calvary *physically*. So everything that happened in the life of Christ physically was written eternally. Surely, He perfected every counsel.

> *When Jesus saw that everything that was written of Him was fulfilled, having accomplished them all, He said it is finished.* **John 19:28-30**

Paul the apostle concluded His choreographed life by saying I have run the race, I have fought the good fight, in other words, I have finished *that* which was required of me. May you believe there is nothing you are doing today, that was not planned to be done in a certain way, that you may fulfill the perfect will of God for your life. The choreography of purpose is the reason why revelation from God concerning your life is available and necessary, that you might know what is required of you in the land of the living. For as many as are led by the Spirit shall walk confidentially through the ordained pathways of God; *the power of one person in the journey of a lifetime.*

You don't make purpose to be fulfilled but rather purpose was designed to fulfill you. It gives you the identity of your inclusion in God's master plan.

Thereafter awaits for you in heaven, a brilliant embrace from the Lord and Savior, Jesus Christ the head of the Church and the preeminence of all things. As you meet in eternity, with His embrace comes an eye-to-eye interlocking of joy between you and God as a graduate of His *School of Purpose* while you were on the earth. He probably will remove your mantle, which He gave to you, for your work on this earth. What a day to behold! This truth is accurate for all called to this journey with destiny in God. It is however a dimension of heightened life through a demography never seen before in a thousand lifetimes. This kind of road map is too sophisticated for your understanding – *You must be schooled unto fulfillment.*

I Corinthians 12:7 declares that the Spirit of the Lord in whom God's gifts, administrations and operations, are manifest, makes everybody to profit. It is important to understand that there is no fulfillment of God's purpose in this earth without His Holy Spirit encountering a mortal being yielded to God. Without the Holy Spirit there is no tangible fulfillment in God's business world. Jesus said at the age of twelve, I should be after my Father's business. Using a marketplace vocabulary of "business" which reflects profit and loss, manufacturing, creativity and advancement, He is therefore saying, *I was brought into this earth for the singular business of purpose;* so should be the module of every God-loving child.

> **Our business is God's purpose and**
> **God's purpose is our business.**

I, even I, have spoken; yea, I have called him: I have brought him, and he shall make his way prosperous. Come ye near unto me, hear ye this; I have not spoken in secret from the beginning; from the time that it was, there am I: and now the Lord God, and his Spirit, hath sent me. Thus saith the Lord, thy Redeemer, the Holy One of Israel; I am the Lord thy God which teacheth thee to profit, which leadeth thee by the way that thou shouldest go.

Isaiah 48:15-17

The Old Testament summary of God's business and profit margin is summarized in Isaiah 48:17:

- I am the Lord your God, your Redeemer and the Holy One of Israel
- Which teaches you to profit
- Which leads you in the prosperous way that you should go

Coming into terms with this scripture brings our investigation of God's *School of Purpose* to rest. It is a true matter that God does not speak in secret, as to just to an exclusive person to profit and to leave the rest in poverty. God invites all from the North Pole to the South Pole, to draw close to Him and to be instructed and helped in His *School of Glory and Purpose*. I pray you enroll yourself today by simply saying, "Lord Here Am I, use me and send me." May you be the formidable student of God like this world has never seen before. May you be a prodigy of the Most High and a royal standard-bearer to our generation.

In the time of Joshua, God invites him into the *School of Purpose*:

> *Now after the death of Moses the servant of the Lord it came to pass, that the Lord spake unto Joshua the son of Nun, Moses' minister, saying, Moses my servant is dead; now therefore arise, go over this Jordan, thou, and all this people, unto the land which I do give to them, even to the children of Israel. Every place that the sole of your foot shall tread upon, that have I given unto you, as I said unto Moses. From the wilderness and this Lebanon even unto the great river, the river Euphrates, all the land of the Hittites, and unto the great sea toward the going down of the sun, shall be your coast. There shall not any man be able to stand before thee all the days of thy life: as I was with Moses, so I will be with thee: I will not fail thee, nor forsake thee. Be strong and of a good courage: for unto this people shalt thou divide for an inheritance the land, which*

I swore unto their fathers to give them. Only be thou strong and very courageous, that thou mayest observe to do according to all the law, which Moses my servant commanded thee: turn not from it to the right hand or to the left, that thou mayest prosper withersoever thou goest. This book of the law shall not depart out of thy mouth; but thou shalt meditate therein day and night, that thou mayest observe to do according to all that is written therein: for then thou shalt make thy way prosperous, and then thou shalt have good success. Have not I commanded thee? Be strong and of a good courage; be not afraid, neither be thou dismayed: for the Lord thy God is with thee whithersoever thou goest. **Joshua 1:1-9**

It is an amazing picture to behold in your spirit as to how God would invite a student into the principal's office and presents to him his purpose or assignment with clearly defined instructions and educational curriculum and structure for a success higher than the best of man's brain power. If God is your principal in your journey of destiny of leadership, then I will say, you are an accomplished, off-the-chart success story about to be revealed.

- Be courageous, He said, and every place the sole of your foot shall tread, that has already been given to you.
- Be courageous, He said, no man shall be able to stand before you all the days of your life.
- Be courageous, He said, with strength you will divide

167

the inheritance of the land to the people, according to promise and prophecy.

- Be courageous, He said, to observe all the law which Moses gave unto you.
- Be courageous, He said, and turn not to the right or to the left, that you may be prosperous wherever you go, with the strength of focus.
- Be courageous, He said, that thou meditate in the word day and night and stick to this book of the law, keep the words of the scriptures in your mouth
- With COURAGE meditate day and night, consistently and
- With COURAGE observe to do all that is written.
- Be courageous, He said, and make your way prosperous to obtain good success.

God concludes His lecture in verse nine by saying, "*Have I not commanded thee?*"

- Be strong
- Be of good courage
- Be not afraid
- Do not be dismayed
- For the Lord thy God is with you wherever you go as a Sovereign.

A classroom lecture of this type to a master student in God's Kingdom faculty, can only set you above and above only all the days of your life. Truly purpose draws you into the world of God's highways. It is a high life. Whatever you keep to yourself you lose, but whatever you release into God's hands you gain. It is the Lord's highway. Only the brave, strong, courageous, obedient and yielded walk it. This is who you are.

A DAILY WALK

This subject of your obedience takes you through a learning process of a lifetime. The daily walk with God is a virtual instructed equation. You are on your own to do whatever you like, without a God-centered focus, but the moment you yield your life to Him, you follow the syllabus and curriculum of His word which directs you into His will and without which you cannot locate His ways.

Purpose can be defined as the reason for which something exists or is done, made, used, etc. It is also an intended or desired result, aim, goal or end. There is a determination and resoluteness that makes the subject complete in all its setting. The connection between purpose and its schooling is as a result of God's presentation of the subject in His Kingdom.

> *Having made known unto us the mystery of his will, according to his good pleasure which he hath purposed in himself: That in the dispensation of the fullness of times he might gather together in one all things in Christ, both which are in heaven, and which are on earth; even in him.* **Ephesians 1:9-10**

Ephesians reveals that the purpose of God is derived from His will and pleasure, that in the fullness of time, he might gather in ONE all things in heaven and earth. To consider the mystery in assembling all things into ONE purpose is significant. Which means if that one person failed then all things of God and in God, could be destroyed. The subject of purpose is complex and extremely serious. This is the eternal purpose of God of which we all locate our identity or relevance in Christ. The truth is, if purpose is a derivative of His perfect will and absolute pleasure then it must be a very tall order; that is to say of the most esteemed standard and key, too high for anyone to attain. It is also too complex for our comprehension without His help. Learning to fly an airplane is far more simple compared to managing the purpose of God without help; it is that critical. Having said so, since He is a Jealous Sovereign God who will not throw His glory away carelessly, but guard and protect it, so is His purpose very personal to Him. If you mishandle the subject of purpose, you literally touch the very pupil of His eye and the core of His person.

Romans 8:28 presents four factors:

1. All things work together for the good

2. To them that love God

3. To them that are called

4. According to His purpose

Meaning because of His purpose, He will surely cause nothing to fail around those that are called, and choose to love what

He loves. Your love is proved by your unconditional obedience and sacrifice. When He has an assignment for you He has the purpose and the calling in His hand, but you have the love and the diligence in your heart. Focusing on what He wants from you can be a proof of your love to what is dear to Him and surety that nothing good or bad stops you. If purpose is reflective of His pleasure then anyone who apprehends purpose receives His pleasure. He is well pleased with anyone who becomes one with His purpose. Of Christ He said, "This is My beloved Son in whom I am well pleased." Christ had the same choices we face today, but focused on nothing else but that which He knew is the dearest value to His Father.

If purpose is His pleasure then failure is His displeasure.

Being so complex yet made simple through Christ, that as we live in Christ on a daily basis, we attract God's pleasure even as Christ pleased Him. I will say for you to live and move and have your being in Christ on a daily basis, is to enter center stage of His heart's pleasure. Once I am in Christ, I am in His pleasure.

Welcome to God's pleasure on a daily basis! – *His Purpose.*

In my personal life I remember vividly the day after I received Jesus into my heart as Lord and savior. Coming from a family background in the manufacturing industry and business, with a father who was politician and once a member of parliament, I had a different concept of God as a Presbyterian. The week I had my personal encounter with Christ Jesus, little did I know that I had just stepped into the purpose of God for my life. As

171

Paul said, "All purpose is found in Christ." When I began to live and move and have my being in Him, I had a strong sense of peace and a consciousness that I was now connected to the right pathway for which cause I was born.

It is usually very difficult to explain in human words the experience of a mortal suddenly connecting to the invisible eternal pathway laid out for him or her. It just feels right and it felt right for me too. The joy of apprehending the course of life for me was overwhelming. There was such a clear difference between my experience from the home and parenting in which I was born, and the new home of Christ's Kingdom, into which I was born again. The experience was almost like traveling from one planet to the other and discovering what had already been prepared for me over the years, which would have been impossible to attain, had I not gone through the way, the truth and the life Christ Jesus My Savior, coach and role model.

THE PREVIOUS AND THE NOW

Saul of Tarsus found His purpose in the most dramatic way as did Moses by the burning bush. These two biblical characters were pillars in their days, who had graphic crossover pathways, whose experiences from the old and the new characterize the two different natures and their purposes. The old nature has its purpose in human devices but the new nature, in the purpose of God. As Moses killed for righteousness in his thinking, which made him a fugitive, so Saul also persecuted and killed for His conviction which was also a man made devise. Both these *old na-*

tures believed they were right and so it is today. There are several religious beliefs that think convincingly as doing a good thing until they encounter the Spirit of God's purpose. It is amazing how in God's divine time He knows exactly how to connect an individual into His sovereign will. He is God who never loses.

Both Moses and Paul had a *crack-down* from God's eternal master plan. Rescued by destiny and pulled violently out of cemented-hard rock of human devices into the Kingdom of God's purpose where stony hearts of rebellion are transformed into hearts of flesh and goodness. The end result of these two gentlemen was that they both became very meek and trail-blazed a brand new order of life, not just for their generation but for the entire human race, forever. God is not looking for tough vessels, but broken vessels. He does not use rocks, He uses clay. He knows how to turn a rock into an earthen vessel for the purpose of establishing His original plan. He is God. He is the boss. He says, "I know the thoughts I have towards you, to give you a hope and a future, then you shall call upon Me and I will answer you."

It is vividly clear that both Moses and Saul - who were pillars of faith in their time - connected to a pathway of life that had not been experienced before. They illuminated a fresh pathway ordained by God. God has *THE WAY* for every destined individual in leadership.

Saul, with an identity of riotous, rough persecutor with a legal mind, had lots of murderous records in his life. *He framed mischief by a law;* that was the image attached to the name Saul of Tarsus. He was among the bad boys, literally a highly educated *bad man*. Sometimes we think that proper education is privilege to a license to fight God with audacity. The truth is, Moses was equally highly educated and in today's education, probably was a professor of humanities. The encounter between these two gentlemen and God was a headlong collision of the divine power of love, against human sophistication at its best.

To imagine that God would still have a plan for a human being that will may so far away from the divine nature, is an intriguing revelation of the strength of purpose from God's heart. I do believe that before the foundation of the world Saul was created to be a vessel of God but somehow, as it has been in the life of many, the fall of Adam networked every human into the audacious opposite plan of God for their life. Hence we all start from the negative side, the fallen nature, then we cross over our Red Sea into the positive in Christ, which is ultimately the original reason of our life and existence. In other words but for the fall of man, there would be no need for a rebirth of being *born again*. As it is important for every person to come through the womb of a woman into the earth, so it is imperative for every person to be born again through the womb of the Holy Spirit into a new nature; the true purpose of God.

In Acts 9:1-18 Saul is on his journey to persecute the people of *The Way* in Damascus. Christianity today was originally called *The Way*. Truly it is the way of God into eternal life. As Christ is the way, the truth and the life (John 14:6) so are we connected to this highway of saints. The culture of God is revealed in this pathway: *The Way*. Everybody who will see God face to face in eternity must locate this way. In this great clout of tormenting *The Way*, in Acts 9, heaven opens up and descends upon Saul in the person of Jesus Christ, the Messiah. Struck down by the Light of *The Way*, Jesus Christ, it is believed that Saul was lifted off his stallion eight feet above his horse, onto the ground. Saul of Tarsus, the rock, crushed that day onto the ground and became a softened piece of clay ready to be remolded on the wheel of the Potter's house. Paul the Apostle was birthed at that spirit-time.

> *But the Lord said unto him, Go thy way: for he (Paul) is a chosen vessel unto me, to bear my name before the Gentiles, and kings, and the children of Israel.* **Acts 9:15**

Jesus the eternal purpose of God, the Person of The Way, the Redeemer of the whole world, refers to Paul as a chosen vessel who had to be instructed to fulfill what had been ordained for him before the foundation of the world (Acts 9:15-18). The principle of the crushing of the hard rock Saul to become the meek Apostle Paul and revelator, is synonymous of how God takes the clay and molds a vessel into gold for glory and honor unto Himself. This was an absolute rebirthing into the purpose designed for him. Saul of Tarsus was the devise of man. Paul of Tarsus became the purpose of God. In between the two natures and all the way into eternity, is a journey of the *School of Purpose* everybody must enroll into.

Moses the Hebrew son of Pharaoh's daughter became Moses the prophet of God. Both of these gentlemen received the oracles of God. In the Old Testament on Mount Sinai from Moses who use to be a murderer and from Paul with approximately 75% of what was written in the New Testament involved his ministry work; Paul being a previous murderer as well. These two pillars, one in the old, one in the new, between the two of them, they changed the world of worship, priesthood and servitude under God; *the power of one.* If there is one thing that is common between these two guys, it is that they exemplified the strength of purpose with a character study that beats all generations in spite of their cultural extremities. God is in business when we connect to His purpose in time. In Philippians 3:12-17, Paul expresses passionately his order in Christ, which became the language of Paul, not of Saul.

> *Not as though I had already attained, either were already perfect: but I follow after, if that I may apprehend that for which also I am apprehended of Christ Jesus. Brethren, I count not myself to have apprehended, but this one thing I do, forgetting those things which are behind, and reaching forth unto those things which are before, I press toward the mark for the prize of the high calling of God in Christ Jesus. Let us therefore, as many as be perfect, be thus minded and if in any thing ye be otherwise minded, God shall reveal even this unto you.*

Nevertheless, whereto we have already attained, let us walk by the same rule, let us mind the same thing. Brethren, be followers together of me, and mark them which walk so as ye have us for an ensample.

Philippians 3:12-17

He said, all I have gained in my past I count but lost honorably, that I might apprehend the purpose for which I was apprehended for on that day to Damascus, and in full consciousness of my purpose I Paul with a brave heart of joy, press in for the prize of the high calling with ONE thing in mind-*I must let go the past!*

Ladies and gentlemen, dear, fellow students of the *College of Purpose*, it is impossible to progress exclusively in the highway of glory designed for you until you are graciously able to disconnect from your past. *It is impossible to hold on to your past and your future at the same time;* that is the crucible of the old nature. But for the revelation of the new, the question becomes, "Why do you look for the living among the dead?"

There is a dead side of every leader, as well as the living side. You need to bury one to give momentum to the other. It's your choice. Your old nature is a dead man. Your new purpose is a living soul. Let go of the dead, it stinks. Arise in the fragrance of the glory laid up for you. Rejoice, again I say rejoice, in the fruitful journey of the school and the college of your purpose. Your singular journey of destiny and leadership in God is underlined right here in the *School of Purpose* with the Holy Ghost as your professor. His purpose is the reason why He made us to live and move and have our being in Him.

CHALLENGES

God has created everything in heaven and on the earth to advance His purpose in your life without fail. There is therefore a reason why the enemy goes after people of purpose. Show me purpose driven individuals and I can tell you who the enemy desires to destroy; because of the preciousness of God's purpose in His heart He certainly defuses the enemy's ploy to destroy us at all times. What is at stake? It's not you, but the purpose you carry and represent.

In Job 1:3-10 God is incredibly enthused by Job's character of purpose. It was the very life Job lived and the dream he lived for. As you lay hold of God's purpose and run effectively, you will *make God's day* for a lifetime.

- Persecution is what the devil brings your way in attempting to stop you from fulfilling your purpose.
- A trial is what you go through based on the natural difficulties that attempt to inhibit your obedience and journey.

Fulfilling God's plan for your life on the earth that to say, on this part of creation, is to face different, natural inhibitions that are not in heaven. No matter how righteous you are, you need to overcome every obstacle and prevail by the power of God and your faith. To the seven churches of Asia in the first three books of Revelation, Jesus repeatedly pronounces upon the churches, "He that overcomes will I reward." The challenges of the various churches were different, but the key of overcoming was mandatory; so it is for every singular person of purpose for his or her journey of destiny with God.

Many times we confuse trials with persecution. A pregnant lady who goes through the discomfort of nine months and the pain of delivery, experiences the trials of the purpose of bringing a human life into the world. Such a case requires endurance, patience and a strong focus of hope until the end. Hebrews 6:12 says that through faith and patience we inherit the promises, by our diligence.

However sometimes in the midst of your trials, there can be an attack of the enemy, hoping to abort the purpose of God. For instance the disciples obeyed Christ to enter the boat and cross the Sea of Galilee. In their obedience of sailing though the waters - not an easy task to begin with - there came a contrary wind with a torpedo instinct to destroy the leadership team of Jesus. That was persecution from the devil but at that same time their faith to overcome was under trial.

Many times our faith is on trial, either by the persecution of the devil, or by the growth processes of God. Being able to handle these storms, drives home the value of maturity in trusting God no matter the origin of the challenge. The end result of this challenging process enables you to experience the glory of God's grace upon every singular individual in the journey of destiny and leadership. Since the disciples were under the covering of the Messiah, He became their present help in time of trouble. The journey of purpose is a *School of Instruction* because of the complexities of the syllabus and the curriculum, which no one else can put together, but the Author and the Finisher of our faith.

Both the syllabus and the curriculum of your purpose are deeply established in the mind and heart of God. For this cause His expectation of your obedience is for the issues of His heart to be downloaded into your spirit. This empowers you to run your race and finish your assignment according to His will. It is essential therefore that His Holy Spirit teach you in this great *School of Purpose.* You need Him as your Paraclete for He is the one that comes alongside you on your journey.

CHAPTER 19:

THE KEY OF THE SPIRIT

The disciples of Jesus, being the future apostles, had a difficult time in their school of purpose and destiny while following Jesus. Their challenges included:

1. Their inability to perform the miracles and teach as their leader did.

2. Their inability to comprehend His separation from them through death, burial and eventual resurrection.

Accepting their challenges, it was tough for the disciples to assimilate the information at this juncture. This puzzle being fixed, Jesus introduced the expediency of another Comforter who would come from heaven to be in them and with them on their journey. The Comforter therefore answered their questions and restored their confidence in the days after. Behold, the disciples took the purpose of God from Jerusalem, Judea, Samaria, and to the uttermost parts of the earth.

> *Peace I leave with you, my peace I give unto you: not as the world giveth, give I unto you. Let not your heart be troubled, neither let it be afraid.*

John 14:27

This scripture creates the true atmosphere that needs to surround leadership, to give insightfulness for everyone's pathway. The unknown future to the *disciple-leaders* was the reason for their fear. Fixing that problem, in those days, is the key to solving the same challenge of all times. Lack of knowledge can develop fear of the unknown, but the right knowledge and revelation produces awareness and hope for the future. The right vision is given when the Holy Spirit comes. Jesus said in John 14:1-16 That I will pray the Father and He will send down the Comforter, whose indwelling in you will make you do greater works than this. The Holy Spirit is the *key* to the right revelation needed by every individual on their journey of destiny and purpose; *the power of one man.*

John 14:16 calls the Holy Spirit a:
- Counselor
- Helper
- Intercessor

- Advocate

- Strengthener

- Standby

In the absence of knowledge to any subject there are losses, fear and innocence but to a large degree, ignorance. The key to receiving knowledge from God is designed by the process of the Holy Spirit coming along side you on a daily basis and being a part of all that you are and all that you do until the end. He is the supernatural Advocate for your purpose.

Keys are vital. Losing the keys to your house, car, or bank vault is to shut the door to your treasure. Losing the Holy Spirit is the shutting of the gates to your glory and purpose. Having Him on your side is having access to joy and fulfillment. Truly it doesn't get any better than this, when both you and Him become inseparable. You will be considered in your journey on this earth, as a person *wondered at* and a thorough phenomenon to observe in *the power of one.* It is at that stage that one can be considered as a person in God who is "bigger than life" and all the circumstances that come with it.

Ladies and gentlemen, to have dominion in this world, you must be bigger than life. How possible is this? It is very simple. If Jesus can give you life and life more abundantly then He is giving you a package far much larger then the normal existence of life. The *much more abundantly* equation extends to you the divine lifestyle; a chemistry which takes your performance ratio far above human levels. You are called a vessel of honor unto God, exceeding all expectations by the key of the Spirit that dwells mightily within you. The Holy Spirit is the achiever that dwells within ordinary people to produce extraordinary results; *The Power of One*.

The book of Exodus shows how close God and Moses were as friends on this journey of purpose. Completely overwhelmed by this incredible God and seeing all the great and creative miracles of a thousand years crammed into one person's lifetime, the prophet Moses was in awe. At one point in time he couldn't handle it anymore and said, "Oh God, show me Your ways that I might know You!" To enjoy the journey with God you must experience His awe. Yes, every single person in the school of purpose must break into the synergy of His awe. There always comes a time when you get overwhelmingly hungry to know Him. Your hunger to know Him must be so much more then your desire to produce results. A student of God's wise ways makes you wise and a servant in His glorious presence makes you thirst for His glory. In other words, you become who you worship and you desire to be like him who is your teacher (if he is a good teacher). In this case there is no better teacher than God. Moses said, "Lord, don't take your presence from me because my identity has become a transformed creation of Your presence. My identity is ruined outside your presence. If I the leader of this people cannot have your presence, then I am disqualified to lead them in your name." Not satisfied, Moses presses the next button by requesting of God to show him His glory.

God's opinion about the gentleman Moses was revealed in

Numbers 12:3-8 and had called Moses was very meek, above all men on the earth. The Lord said I speak to Moses face to face because of his faithfulness in my house. Exodus 33:9-23 states that:

- Moses was a friend of God
- He desired the way of God
- He was a man of the presence of God
- He was separated unto God
- He desired to bask in the glory of God
- He enjoyed the goodness, the mercy and the graciousness of God
- He had insight into God exclusively

Deuteronomy 34:7-12 states that:

- Moses was 120 years old and in perfect physical condition
- Moses was a man God knew face to face
- He walked in signs and wonders before the people of God and Pharaoh
- The might and the terror of God functioned through him

In all these listed attributes of Moses' fellowship and intimate ministry with God (which is an incredible pathway for every leader of destiny) is this theme, "The Key of the Spirit." We must desire this.

Paul says in 1 Corinthians 12:7, that the manifestation of the

Spirit is for every man to profit. By the full manifestation of the Holy Ghost in your life, you have all that Moses enjoyed and so much more. Based on what we have today with the Holy Ghost makes all that Moses experienced look very inconclusive. This is your time to enjoy the express works of the Holy Spirit. In all that you do, let Him guide you and in all that He does, He will involve you. I perceive the Spirit of God yearning earnestly to take you over on your journey. In Acts 8:27-31 Philip was inspired to join the Ethiopian eunuch traveling from Jerusalem to Ethiopia. The Holy Ghost draws close to every person on the journey of purpose that would invite Him into their chariot. He is waiting for your vital invitation. If it is His pleasure to do so, then it must be yours to accept Him. Let Him to take you over. Enjoy the ride in the passenger seat.

I perceive the Holy Ghost drawing close to you also in such a manner that if you will let Him, He will come alongside you on this journey of destiny and leadership. I pray a strong, intimate spirit to Spirit fellowship with the Spirit of God in all your journey. He is the key; *The Power of One in the intimate fellowship with the Holy Ghost.*

In I Corinthians 2:9-12 we see how important it is for the Holy Spirit, who searches the deep things of God, to be our Paraclete and Helper. This is because every singular person's calling is to discover in our natural world "what eyes have not seen nor ear heard, neither ever entered our hearts, what God as for us." This means on our journey of purpose there is a consistent revelation discovered as we turn the wheels of God's heart

186

through our obedience. Plans and deep intentions which already exist in heaven are inspired into our hearts to be unveiled into this world. Whereas every generation has a plan of God to be fulfilled, individual callings in God become the conduit through which, what generations must know, is revealed for manifestation. We discover many more things as we avail ourselves as intimate vessels with the Holy Spirit. Eyes have not seen, ears have not heard, neither has it ever entered the heart of man, but are revealed when God finds yielded vessels of purpose.

> *But as it is written, Eye hath not seen, nor ear heard, neither have entered into the heart of man, the things which God hath prepared for them that love him. But God hath revealed them unto us by his Spirit. For the Spirit searcheth all things, yea, the deep things of God. For what man knoweth the things of a man, save the spirit of man which is in him? even so the things of God knoweth no man, but the Spirit of God. Now we have received, not the spirit of the world, but the spirit which is of God; that we might know the things that are freely given to us of God.* **I Corinthians 2:9-12**

I Samuel 2:35 speaks about how much God desires to raise faithful prodigies to connect to the standards of His heart and mind. The very truth that we are expected to deliver (according to His heart and mind) requires a schooling of instruction and direction in the active duty of purpose. The syllabus and standard set so high – GOD – there must be a curriculum for everyone to follow if we are to achieve His ultimate hope for our calling and mandate. I can understand my personal purpose if I design it, but if He authors His purpose for me, then I need His Spirit to teach me. Every purpose in God's sight must be in the *School of His Spirit*. A great graduation service awaits us all in eternity when all who have succeeded in handling His purpose of grace, will hear the same sentence, "Well done, thou good and faithful servant."

Since advice is the product of the experience of men (from their mind), it is too shallow to help a God designed purpose to succeed. Therefore the deep counsels of the Lord and of leaders who have walked with Him and known His ways, are essential in this educational process of a purpose driven life. The school of purpose keeps teaching you and keeps intriguing you; continually molding you into the image of God. Counsel, therefore creates in you a clean heart of meekness, humility and greatness. Going through the crucibles of His journey turns you into another man with another spirit.

Proverbs 15:22 says without counsel purposes are disappointed but in the multitude of counselors, they are established. This scriptural verse reveals two personalities: the personality of God who is the counsel and the personality of leaders, seniors, patriarchs and matured saints. This scripture also means, where there is no true counsel of God, every purpose is disappointed. May we be sensitive to the inspirations of the Lord as He orders our steps and makes us prudent and productive in this lifetime. The power of one in the hand of God the counselor, is a success story. The ultimate result of your life is determined by the loving God whose grace is sufficient to make us succeed in spite of all odds.

If Isaiah 46:9-11 states that God declares the end from the beginning then it means that God has known the successful picture of your journey; that He has made you successful therefore He can instruct you to fulfill what has already been a successful project. In other words your obedience makes you an accomplished leader before the journey began. You are a success about to happen without fail; *The School of Purpose*. It is a conclusive equation it is not what you know nor how prepared you are, but who you know intimately, the Holy Ghost as your personal Counselor.

CHAPTER 20:

THE HONOR OF SUFFERING

It is often said, "If it doesn't hurt, it doesn't work." To suffer can be defined as: to undergo, be subjected to, or endure pain, distress, injury, loss or anything unpleasant. It is by all standards a very uncomfortable state of being at any time or anywhere. Contrary to expectation these former students of Christ - now on their own as apostles - took an admirable stand. In Acts 5:40-42 after being beaten by the authorities, the apostles went rejoicing that they were counted worthy to suffer shame for the name of Christ.

Suffering, as difficult as it has always been, can be much more endured if there is a reasonable cause or purpose for it. The apostles after having gone through unwarranted harassment and emotional distress for no wrongdoing, were also beaten by authorities for no proper legal cause. Being subjected to this embarrassment publicly, they went about rejoicing. Should one mourn or rejoice in the wake of shame? The decision is relative to the individual level of maturity and insightfulness of every one singular person. If you are not able to handle shame effectively, you will probably not be qualified to maintain success and glory. The process of shame and its learning curves builds in you the appreciation, value, and the essence of good success.

There is no suffering in heaven. It is a place of blissful glory with an unimaginable absence of pain. Jesus said, "In My Father's house there are many mansions and I go to prepare a place for you, and when I'm done, I will come and take you there (John 14:1-2)." He said, "Let not your heart be troubled." Troubles are here on earth and therefore the place of all who have fallen short of the glory of God because of the fall of mankind. The curse - because of the fall -brought sorrows on all women in childbirth. The curse brought suffering. The systems of this earth and the suffering which invaded its systems shall not end until the end of this world gives way to the New Jerusalem.

Many dimensions of sufferings and discomfort are alleviated and in some cases reduced to bare minimum or even blocked out as circumstances change based on the enactment of certain principles of God. It is important to receive the help of the Lord, through all the days of every human life, to overcome. Being born again and walking in the ways of God has been the wisest pathway. This is because going through suffering, because of a fallen world, is a tough and unbearable journey. Through Christ an extraordinary grace and help from the Holy Spirit strengthens each individual. Through Christ, we are delivered by the redemptive power of the blood of Jesus from the curse which has fed the suffering. As much as we don't have to accept the curse of the natural world and its spiritual pressures, we have a role to play in renewing our minds by accessing the provisions made by the Holy Spirit to teach, help and transform us into what the Bible says we are, which is *overcomers and more than conquerors.*

There are natural and spiritual laws of life. In the natural certain things don't change because of the human society made up of the independent will of people's choices; some bad, some worse, some unacceptable. These choice elements, if not guided by the love of God, create systems of trouble for others. The ripple effect of human errors due to ungodly intentions, ignorance, or in some cases immaturity and lack of knowledge have contributed to the challenge of suffering. Freedom through Christ, because He paid for our sins, removing the curse of the law, brings us into the wavelength of a true Spirit-led life. Yes, it is possible to have the joy of the Lord as our strength so as to navigate our way favorably and with confidence.

One might ask, "If Christ paid it all, why do we still experience suffering?"

Here is the answer: The finished work of the cross is a done deal. The repair, provision and full restoration of the original plan of God for man is conclusive. It is therefore a provision, connected to principles that as many that can lay hold on these principles, believe them and walk the pathway laid, can enjoy what is provided. The result of the victory on the cross does not however negate the principles of pain that the human race holds on to. There are certain aspects however of the suffering equation which help us overcome the prideful nature of the human flesh that must continually be worked on and kept out of the way of our fellowship with God. Breaking the mold of habitual living outside the high profile and yet simple principles of Christ, requires the discipline of consistently reversing ungodly trends and norms. This conflict creates suffering. Suffering can cause you to break out of mediocrity into the superfluous highlife of God or yielding to the wickedness of the enemy, his torture, oppression, repression or destruction.

In John 10:10, Jesus said, "The devil comes to kill, steal and destroy." This three-fold conspiracy of darkness inflicts suffering and damnation. On the contrary the proposal of Christ and His mission statement is to overwhelm evil with amazing goodness and success. For the three plans of darkness (kill, steal, destroy) God has given us three keys (He has come, to give, abundant life).

Christ	Devil
Has Come	To Kill
To Give	To Steal
Abundant Life	To Destroy

For the three fold-purpose of the enemy, Christ has released His three dimensional supreme plan to neutralize:

- He came to abort the killing instincts of darkness.
- He has given His life in replacement for all the things stolen and robbed from the human race with the purpose of reducing the glory of man to nothingness and poverty.
- Christ overwhelmed all the destructive programs of darkness, with His abundant light of life.

These keys put us far above all principalities and powers, making us rule and reign in absolute victory. The key of accepting Christ into your life and the gift of God that He is to us, explains the relevance of the Kingdom. With these we outwit the schemes of darkness designed to stop every man from fulfilling his God-given purpose. It's a gift of God to choose abundant life, choose the ways of Christ, and receive eternal rest in Him. The salvation we receive separates our spirit from any form of suffering, being born again in the Holy Spirit.

Our soul, comprised of our mind, will, and emotions, is being renewed daily to the extent that we enforce the Word of God according to the will of God. Meditation on the word and its application in obedience sets you free from the law of sin and death. Where as the suffering from the principles of the enemy bring condemnation and ultimate destruction, Christ came to set us free and there is now therefore no condemnation if we choose to believe it. The greatest part of suffering though rests within the carnal realm; the inter-activity of the natural realm of the flesh, our soul: the mind, will and emotions. Our attachment to the accrued experience of natural crave without God's instruction create strong bonding with vanity whose detachment, for the sake of purity in God, creates pain and emotional destabilization. Suffering can be experienced from denying your flesh what it has become so use to or to suddenly quit loving what the Holy Spirit dislikes.

Culture is developed in the natural realm of consistent agreement of human ways, but with the Holy Spirit, you are connecting to a *divine nature*, which is different from culture. Both words end with "ture" (nature, culture) but are absolutely poles apart. By the help of the Holy Spirit, the *cultural arrest* is broken into the divine nature of eternal, life-bearing fruit, pleasing to our God. This transition creates suffering. Suffering is can be seen as a fight between our accepted cravings versus walking in the fruit of the Holy Spirit, such as love.

Being extremely passionate about worldly success and its accolades in culture, Apostle Paul's experience of freedom from the earthly weights of life granted him the unprecedented zeal-power to break loose from the old to obtain the new knowledge and nature of Christ. What Christ gave him spiritually had to be made fruitful by overcoming the flesh and its desires. Paul said, "That I may lay hold onto to that which I was arrested by (God's love). To attain, even paying the price and pressing in for the high calling and the best life. (Philippians 3:6-14)." The strong words of *"letting go of his past"* is the revealed key to every singular one person on this journey of fulfilling the one purpose of your destiny and leadership. Letting go of the weaknesses of the past and its fleshly control, to obtain the liberty of His sweet Spirit.

Philippians 2:5-11 reveals how even Jesus had to humble himself unto death, setting the prototype for every each individual to follow. Compared to the ultimate victory, it is worth the package. Gird your loins and renew your mind on the subject of suffering.

> *Let this mind be in you, which was also in Christ Jesus: Who, being in the form of God, thought it not robbery to be equal with God: But made himself of no reputation, and took upon him the form of a servant, and was made in the likeness of men: And being found in fashion as a man, he humbled himself, and became Wherefore God also hath highly exalted him, and given him a name which is above every name: That at the name of Jesus every knee should bow, of things in heaven, and things in earth, and things under the earth; that every tongue should confess that Jesus Christ is Lord, to the glory of God the Father.* **Philippians 2:5-11**

The creation process of man caused God to pronounce five expectations in Genesis 1:28:

- Be fruitful
- Multiply
- To replenish

- Subdue

- Have dominion

The essential establishment of these five attributes, are always surrounded by pain and challenges. With dominion as its ultimate goal, those who attain it always have a story to tell and it hasn't always been a bed of roses. For the apostles to consider it a worthy cause to suffer for the name of Christ, is to say they were privileged in entirety. Defining the reason for the pain can make you smile through the distress, knowing full well there is profit beyond the current situation. Life sometimes throws a curve ball at you but your attitude of response makes all the difference. You may not be able to control the behavior of others or a system but your perception and response lies within your control. I think instead of pursuing a lawsuit for revenge, the apostles probably made a good decision to rejoice. If the devil wants to see you cry, kindly disobey him and rejoice. Endeavor to make it impossible for the enemy to think that he got you where it hurts. The hope of your calling is the clear understanding that pain announces a fruitful future. It also brings you into the category of the overcomers.

Identifying with the greatness of Jesus, the apostles consider it not robbery to keep their focus and vision in the midst of suffering and shame. To be punished for a cause, is to be identified for the same. They said, its about time society considers us as members of Christ's lifestyle other than the opposite. They rejoiced because their pain proved that they were not hypocrites in the way of the Lord but absolutes in their belief. A woman in her time of pregnancy goes through distressing seasons, but in the rejoicing of bringing life, she endures the pain until the end. It is truly a privilege to suffer for a good cause. What you cannot die for is not worth living for. On this journey of destiny as one man, unfavorable circumstances may come your way but remember that they come to prove your worth and inclusion in this unique style of life.

In 1 Corinthians 16:9 Paul announces that adversities, many times, gravitate towards open doors of great opportunities and great gain. So long as God allows the earth to be governed by physical and spiritual laws intermittently, suffering and unfairness shall continue. It is the product of the flaws found in the state of man. Heaven, having no flaws in its citizens, is therefore a planet devoid of suffering. Suffering is created by human weaknesses and sin. It can be said that the attacks of the enemy, persecutions, trials and personal errors create atmospheres of suffering and shame, but the pain inflicted is usually through the weakness that exists in us. Persecution takes more toll on the aggregate of weakness and less impact on the strong. In stormy weather the eagle locks its wings and flies into higher heights against the contrary wind, but the weaker birds struggle. For the apostles to rejoice was a sign of strength. As one individual person called, I pray that you will be strong in the days of adversity and keep your hope alive. Some of the reasons why Paul would say that adversities surround great doors of opportunity is because there are many vying for the same privilege, with greater desperation then you can imagine.

Secondly, it is Satan's insatiable dream to stop effectual doors opened by God because of the glory attached. For every great door opened, there is a success story that is constantly designed to lift up the good name of the Lord. In the event that a person's purpose or great door of opportunity is destroyed, the good name of the Lord is dared into disrepute. Open doors activate God's awesome glory. Obedience to fight through provokes His unusual presence and majesty. Keep wining over shame and reproach and continue piling up and increasing testimonies to God's name and glory. He is a good God and deserves our sacrifices of endurance with great pleasure. Your calling is an opportunity, your purpose is an open door and your victory is a celebration of God's greatness and omnipotence. So you can imagine when God gives it to you, envy comes along side from those who wish they had it but couldn't. For example, the fall of Lucifer was the failure of his purpose for which cause our success in obeying God magnifies God's justice for kicking him out of heaven. Your success story is bad news to the archenemy of God. Small minded people fight good people doing greater things as a sign of their weakness and insecurity. The devil's ability to inflict pain and torture is a sign of his weakness against God.

Romans 8:16-19 says the Spirit of God bears witness that we are the sons of God, therefore heirs and joint heirs with Christ the King. The proof of heirdom is the capital of heritage assigned. As sons of God we inherit all that Christ is and all He has. In Paul's admonishment to the church of Rome, he fruitfully connects the glory of Jesus to its suffering. To the church of Corinth he compares great open doors to adversity, but in our state of being in Christ, suffering comes along side the exceptional blissfulness we attain in Christ.

> *For I consider that the sufferings of this present time are not worthy to be compared with the glory which shall be revealed in us.* **Romans 8:18**

Suffering could also be the disciplines of the physical flesh in managing the spiritual blessing, calling and responsibilities. It is a glorious thing when your ministry is catering for masses, whose needs are overwhelming. With this weight of responsibility upon your shoulders, many depend on your ability to respond to the awesome plan of God upon your life. Many times we are stretched for a good cause, in which case there is suffering that goes along with the glorious success story. Just one example might be that some admirable key leaders sleep only about four hours a night, because of the mandate on their lives. This is the price they pay for their calling. The glory of Jesus, beyond words for value, is often the cause of why our physic goes through breaking points in our response to the heavenly demands of favor. Is Paul therefore suggesting that the endurance of sufferings is weighed alongside the glory? Pretty much so, but much more to say that in the attainment of the fullness of absolute glory in Christ, the existence of any suffering becomes irrelevant. The positive side of suffering - to great movers and shakers - is its ability to keep you sensitive to value and therefore heighten your safety mindedness and security to protect the treasures of God.

> *For the earnest expectation of the creation eagerly*
> *waits for the revealing of the sons of God.*

Romans 8:19

This kind of human living is proven to be an exceptional wonder in all creation for which cause, we get tested and proven for excellence.

I Peter 5:10 says after you have suffered a while you become perfect, established, strengthened and settled. Many times we think suffering and pain is a sign that God is not with you, but in most cases it is rather the sign that you are on track, pushing through the process for the end result of great gain. Every singular person walking in the power of God's will becomes much more solid through the endurance of suffering, becoming effectually fruitful. You are like a fully baked loaf of bread, which is delicious, versus a half-baked one that would not endure the fire to completion. Saints are God's golden vessels that can only be purified by His fire. The more obedient you are in God, the more precious He sees you and the more intimacy He desires of you. Furthermore, your fruitfulness stirs His passion to prune you that you may bear even much more fruit. Every pruning process is a success story in God and demands a sharp edged knife, going into the plant, cutting off undesirables, so that you can blossom even the more. It's an honorable thing to go through this when God desires more of you. It is truly a worthy cause; no wonder the apostles rejoiced. The joy of the Lord, which was activated in them, gave strength to produce more results. Joy in God is not necessarily celebratory but often a proven strength in the wake of adversity.

The sons of God in their full manifestation are suppose to be those who denounce the wickedness of the devil, overcome all systems of controversy and attain the height of grace that brings recovery, redemption and restoration. They in full manifestation are those who give no attention to the enemy's invitation but ride upon the truth of God's pure glory for success. The world today is looking for men and women called of God that would make them forget the pain of their past and focus on the beauty there is. There is a hard-as-diamond thinking process in the spirit of true sons of God, those who see through the fears of the multitude. A hope unshakable is established in their spirits as the anchor of their uncommon success stories, hence the apostles rejoiced for suffering shame for Christ's sake.

> *The eyes of your understanding being enlightened;*
> *that ye may know what is the hope of his calling,*
> *and what the riches of the glory of his inheritance*
> *in the saints, And what is the exceeding greatness of*
> *his power to us-ward who believe, according to the*
> *working of his mighty power.* **Ephesians 1:18-19**

Hope is the key that feeds your endurance through shame and suffering. Suffering therefore is just part of the journey not your destination. Your ability to lay hold of the hope of your calling is based on your understanding of the purpose behind the suffering and its rewards to come. May you identify with the reward of the purpose more then you do with the systems of pain. Receive the strength of mind and unshakable fortitude by the grace of God. The champion of all creation, Christ our Lord and Savior, role modeled the management of pain for a good cause.

> *Wherefore seeing we also are encompassed about with so great a cloud of witnesses, let us lay aside every weight, and the sin which doth so easily beset us, and let us run with patience the race that is set before us, looking unto Jesus the author and finisher of our faith; who for the joy that was set before him endured the cross, despising the shame, and is set down at the right hand of the throne of God.*

Hebrews 12:1-2

In the midst of the cloud of many witnesses, there is a far much more excellent personality, Jesus the author and the finisher of our faith. He set the pace and an incredible standard by enduring the cross and despising its shame and embarrassment, for a far more exceeding glory and coronation as the King of kings and Lord of lords. If He despised the shame to endure the cross then we should do the same. Sometimes unfortunately though, people of destiny are drawn into despising and therefore aborting their future glory by celebrating the pain and the shame. Success through these challenges comes as Christ did which is to denounce and despise the shame. Let go of focusing on the embarrassment (let the Holy Spirit take care of that) and keep pressing in for the prize of the high calling, as one person called of God in this singular journey of purpose and destiny. Jesus took His focus from the shame, suffering and torture and deliberately kept meditating on the joy set before Him. *If God's promises are yea and amen, than your future reward is yea and amen.* May you be the excelling one person in the hand of the God who turns shame into blessing, curses into blessing, challenges into blessing and suffering into even more blessing because of His purpose, which fails not.

CHAPTER 21:

ROLE MODELING

I f it's purpose and transformation then role modeling is relevant. The power of role modeling cannot be underestimated. It sets the tone and the inspiration. It is as a result of the need for focus and connectivity to a pattern. Patterns are extremely essential in both spiritual and physical laws of living:

- It sets the pathways of clarity for the viewer to emulate and improve upon if necessary.

- It sets the dimensions and scopes right and gives insightfulness to what is expected and therefore what it demands.

- It is easier to invest time and energy into what is tangible and understandable.

- It is one of the strong keys for adequate preparation and implementation of purpose, dreams, and visions.

You become a role model when you replicate the best in standards, quality and excellence. If you need one, then you must be one. Role models become points of reference. The subject of the power of one can be related to standard bearing. Whoever has the standard, bears the standard; as much as whoever has the bride has the bridegroom. When God calls a person, in most cases, He sets in order the process of a seed, that is to produce after its own kind into the future. While a patriarch is defined as the head of a family or tribal line, a matriarch is the female of the same. The power of one man is the principle of the institution of patriarchs and matriarchs who become reference points for the generations yet to be born.

The prophet Isaiah relays heaven's ordinance and the endorsement of Abraham's diligence and purpose type setting and declares it is of a great importance to consider the role modeling of achievers in their pursuit for purpose.

> Yes, think about Abraham, your ancestor, and Sarah, who gave birth to your nation. *Abraham was only one man when I called him.* But when I blessed him, he became a great nation.
>
> **Isaiah 51:2 (NLT)**

Look unto Abraham your father, and unto Sarah that bare you: for I called him alone, and blessed him, and increased him.   **Isaiah 51:2 (KJV)**

The Lord God called Abraham all alone, with no practical role model for him to follow but Himself, Jehovah. The obedience of Abraham was therefore imperative and cardinal for he had no other choice and therefore needed to be fully faith-centered and strong. Falling on no one else's contribution for direction he dared not to stagger on the spoken word of God's promises. Obedience took Abraham on his journey to destiny with God faithfully.

The power of one man demands the packaging of the mind, self-will and emotions to maintain straightforward obedience.

The success story of God picking one man such as Abraham, who became the father of faith and the nations, is worth studying and emulating. Faith is the substance of things hoped for; the evidence of things not yet seen. Abraham, without clear tangibility of the future yet without dispute, was persuaded that He who had called him was faithful to accomplish the dream placed in his heart. I can understand how a patriarch of faith became the patriarch of nations under God.

For the Lord shall comfort Zion and will comfort all her waste places and make her wilderness like the Garden of Eden and there shall be joy and gladness found there, thanksgiving and the voice of melody. There is such an incredible joy and gladness and fulfillment that comes into God's world when the one man He chooses walks in obedience. The influence of an obedient person under God's command produces fruit that can transform a barren desert into a flourishing garden, even to the standard of the Garden of Eden. What an amazing comforting principle God has in just finding one person He can use. Everybody who God uses is chosen before time ever began; which means there is always a premeditated decision from God concerning every choice He makes. With the ultimate plan and purpose of transformation. Either a desert becoming a flourishing garden of gladness and joy; producing amazing melodies, or from a prospering state to a much more grandeur fruitfulness and impact. If God can bring so much transformation to the extent of creating a new lineage, as in Abraham's life (the Hebrews), guess what He can do with you, and what He probably *intends* to use you for? You are that incredible, transforming phenomenon that we are about to experience! The power of one man in the hand of God is the key to limitless social transformations in all spheres and layers of the subject.

God, who is perfect in all His ways, has an incredible passion working with imperfect and purposeless people. The strength of His character, His divine nature, as well as His ability to make anything possible, advances His cause in spite of our weaknesses and through the process of time, establishes tremendous and outstanding testimonies of building people to become great standard-bearers of excellence and purpose. The engagement of fellowship between God and man releases influence upon the spirit, soul and body of human vessels of His choice to the intent that it must be known that heavens do rule in the affairs of men.

It is natural for men to fear God and the excellence He walks in, but it is much more glorious to not just fear Him but in humble subservience, trust in His ability to use yielded vessels as partners of destiny and creativity. If God can do anything, then He can use you and I, and our neighbors as well.

It is important to note that as we journey with God on His highway of purpose, two things are essential. The first option is that God can use you to transform other people, societies and generations without you being transformed (if that's what you want). This however is not what God wants. The second option (His preference), is that He would change you to change the world. This is the reason why He encounters individuals that are in His perfect counsel and plan.

On his journey to Damascus, in Acts chapter 9, Saul was encountered by the Lord for the purpose of transforming him by the impact of Christ's blinding light and personality. The strength of engagement between heaven and Saul, recreated him into a new creation, changed his name to Paul and turned him 180 degrees to a totally opposite vision pattern that produced approximately 75% of the works of God to be written in the New Testament. All this was through a transformed vessel.

- We are transformed to transform.
- We are encountered to encounter.
- We are impacted to impact.
- We are led to lead.

The power of one man in the hand of the Creator and Sovereign God is a mystery that even angels look to with great intrigue and delight (Acts 9:4-16).

MEEKNESS

Role modeling is an act of meekness. The greatest leaders have learned how humbling the process is to lead. It requires the selflessness and the outpouring of one's virtues and values into an emptiness and inadequacy that has potential. It is also the process of handling and working on flaws until they become productivities. If you are ready to identify with other's nightmares, with the hope of giving a sure and helping hand with passion, then you are in the right groove for the assignment. Just as many are called for a purpose so also are role models assigned to the job. If your desire is to compete instead of complete then you probably lack maturity. The expectation and standard is for your character to be matured enough to drive purpose into others. A true leader patiently helps people develop character so as to become a purpose driven role model.

Many desire to let others see who they have become and therefore display their self-righteousness. It is true greatness to be small in your own eyes so as to activate potential leaders of tomorrow, who are yet struggling today. Role models seem to have the 20/20 vision as the eagle to locate greatness in the midst of colossal disadvantages as did Christ for us by coming down from the place of excellence into an atmosphere of failure and flaws, to help mold, to the honor of His name, human diamonds of glory. Role models are meek leaders, humble enough to go out of their way, working on mortal minds, continuously sticking with others until they reach the top. It may take years but it's worth it.

Numbers 12:3 says that Moses was the meekest man in the earth and raised incredible leaders and modeled his role with great faithfulness. God said of Moses in verse seven, that he is faithful in all My house. A role model must of necessity be a standard bearer at all times.

Philippians 2:9-11 shows that whereas Christ who was the greatest, humbled Himself through the process of modeling a role for us all by discounting His reputation, implanting into His followers the reputation of excellence, always abounding in good and great works in time and eternity.

> *Wherefore God also hath highly exalted him, and given him a name which is above every name that at the name of Jesus every knee should bow, of things in heaven, and things in earth, and things under the earth; And that every tongue should confess that Jesus Christ is Lord, to the glory of God the Father.*

Philippians 2:9-11

True role models are trusted standard bearers who have great hearts to help where it is needed; even more, help where others are giving up. God always has a different opinion of people we give up on and even sometimes wish never existed. Saul who became Paul would never have had the chance to be an Apostle of Christ if Ananias had convinced God to stay away. Obviously

Ananias lost his chance to spiritually father Paul into greatness. It could have been one of his greatest triumphs in eternal history, had he been able to endure the bad history of Saul by forgiving him and lending a helping hand. No human being can *be too bad to help* by a seasoned role models. If we build physical temples, they will crumple into dust with time, but if we work on mortal minds we brighten eternity with souls as stars brighten the sky. There are many teachers and preachers but not many true, fatherly role models who understand the game.

THE SYLLABUS & CURRICULUM

The priceless contribution to any society anywhere, is to build leaders with a winning character of servitude and sound mind. This should be the dream of every five-star mentor and spiritual father under God's tutelage. As a leader, you are not mentoring a weakness, but unveiling potentials yet to be revealed. Anything less than this is a devaluation of the grace of our Lord Jesus Christ, the love of God and the fellowship of the Holy Spirit. The most successful mentors are those that stick to the grace syllabus with the love and faith curriculum. Be the power of one in the hand of a Sovereign mentor.

God our Creator raises mentors, leaders, pastors, fathers and mothers, delicately because of the strength of glory determined to be revealed in us. The mandate on your life requires the mentor leader you need. Consequently, God selects what kind of person is to be mentored at what time of life. In the prudence of the Most High God, He sometimes puts into the hand of mentors, the future seed of greatness and generational advancers, who at the time are nobodies.

A God ordained mentor needs to be a visionary beyond himself. He also however needs to respect the God given vision of the people being mentored. Many times leaders fall into the snare of aborting or amending God's vision for those who look up to them for help by imposing, what their own interpretation of what they think they should become or due to mishandling of hurts and offenses. Consequently, by mishandling people in our hands, we attempt to edit what God authored about them. It is logical to edit your own script but unlawful to edit God's script about the future of nations and people placed in your custody for a season. Trying to do so, may attempt to dislocate the pathways of both the leader and the students of destiny that go through their hands. Therefore, the greatest attribute of a celebrated mentor is to respect the God given purpose in those around them, even if their future looks more grandeur than the mentor. A steward does not change the rules of the master; so goes the law of stewardship in life.

The coach of a soccer team selflessly invests his life into the players, irrespective whether they become bigger or greater. The joy of every leader should see those who go through their hands so much more successful than themselves. This is a mark of excellence. If God's grace makes us grow from glory to glory, then the same grace makes those who come through the leader's life, increase from glory to glory. As a leader those you raise become your trophies in life before God. They reflect the excellence in you, so the more those around you shine, the more your inner weight of value is reflected. God forbid that the vision of any would die in your hands, as you attend to midwife the birthing of great seed through your role-modeling.

Don't envy your seed. Celebrate them, because for this you were born.

The parable of the eyebrow and the beard throws light to the leader and his student. The student being the beard which grows fast and big yet comes in the later years after the eyebrow's existence. The position of the eyebrow is to protect the eye and vision for the whole body. Without vision the beard would grow long and wild for lack of proper shaping. As a coach should not be envious of a growing child, so the eyebrow has no problem with a growing beard; knowing very well that without the eyebrow's protection of the eye, there is no vision to shape the beard into beauty. The mentor is like the brow that protects the vision for the next generation. Play your God-given role with confidence.

As the bride is the sheep and the groom the shepherd, John makes reference to Jesus as the groom of humanity. This incredible prophet, John the Baptist gladly took steps backwards as the best man for this marriage, to watch it blossom into eternal majesty. A true mentor, coach, spiritual father and leader must enjoy taking steps backwards to advance those who come through their hands. Leaders are first raised to move forward, but in the preparation of the next generation, at the right time of their maturity, they should take steps backwards and make room for their ascendency. Watching them increase more than you is to watch the grandeur of your investment. Their harvest is the crown of your efforts. On their arrival to the top, they eventually make room for their mentors to have a place of rest, covering and rejoicing. In this affect, sons eventually become the covering of their fathers, who covered them when they were immature. So goes the cycle; that which goes around comes around. That which you feed into, feeds into you. The cycle of the journey into destiny is thereby laid bare as a principle and formula which never fails.

Those you lift up will eventually lift you up. Those you bless, bless you. Those you cover, cover you. Those you inspire, inspire you. Those you honor, honor you. This is how the grace that brings glory is processed from generation to generation. This is the school of glory and a genealogy of the seed of God. This is God's family principle. Father's produce great sons who become great fathers.

The champion-leaders you produce through your personal investments, become the books about your values and character that everybody reads.

As you invest virtues into mortal minds, you type your successful purpose in life on the keypad of eternity. There is a large screen of eternal sight and sound that will play the movie of your lifetime with many cheering viewers celebrating your script of success.

As Joseph ended up feeding Jacob; so Christ has brought so much more glory and worship to His father. We are connected to this amazing depth of God's counsel that has kept eternity and time ablaze with the awe of God's goodness. For instance David in the house of Saul was an armor bearer, but if well handled he could have been a major deliverer for King Saul from his dismal ending. He attempted to embarrass David and nail a future messianic patriarch to the wall three times and yet failed. The Bible says that Saul, the father of Jonathan, died on Mount Gilboa, as though he was never anointed by God (1 Samuel 31). Therefore, effective mentoring is a win-win game, built on the principle of "you reap what you sow." King David in his process of life inherited many disgruntled and distressed individuals who were socially rejected.

> *David therefore departed thence, and escaped to the cave Adullam: and when his brethren and all his father's house heard it, they went down thither to him. And every one that was in distress, and every one that was in debt, and every one that was discontented, gathered themselves unto him; and he became a captain over them: and there were with him about four hundred men.* **1 Samuel 22:1-2**

Through the skillful hands of the king, they became the mighty men of David, whose excellence was compared to the effectiveness of angels as in 1 Chronicles 12:22-23. You are a true role model only when you effectively model your role.

Psalm 78:70-72 says, "With integrity of David's heart, he guided them by the skillfulness of His hands." May God give every mentor-leader the prophetic dexterity of skillful hands to turn dismal pictures into glad hearts of generational movers and shakers. Impatience, lack of vision and lack of confidence is the reason why many times we throw the baby out with bathwater.

Who you mentor today can be the hinge to an open door tomorrow. God could also give you a major provider and a future gold mine of a person, in the most unusual package of hopelessness. Failing to harness grace could be a test from God to see what caliber of mentor you are becoming. The more you succeed in mentoring individuals, the higher your grade and value in the Kingdom of saints. In other words, mentors never stop learning and growing in maturity because the syllabus of grace takes you from glory to glory, in the relevance of life's time table.

> *The stone which the builders refused is become the head stone of the corner. This is the Lord's doing; it is marvelous in our eyes.* **Psalm 118:22-23**

Mentorship is one of the marvels of God, when done through the eyes of the Spirit and dexterity of the hands of grace. Always consider the possibility of cornerstones hidden by the chemistry of rejection. Those of the mentor's colony make cornerstones out of rejected pebbles. In conclusion it is important for mentors to be spiritually sensitive to the plans of God for the mentees. What are the chances of this individual being so consistently embarrassed and attacked by the enemy? Is it possibly because the enemy saw a potential cornerstone, that he wishes could be buried and forgotten? It is imperative for mentor leaders to know the voice of the Spirit so as to discern who not to ignore but rather invest into. Our lives are choreographed by the author and the finisher of our faith so if we ask Him, "How do I handle this person?" He will give you the master plan and revelation.

May you excel in your journey to turn the valley of dry bones into a great army of bright shining stars in time and eternity. May we continue to serve the majestic God in whose hand we find power in our singular journey of success in role modeling and Mentorship. May you be the carpenter of the lonely dry wood out there that needs definition and authenticity.

THE FORMULA OF GREATNESS

In John 1:29-30, John the Baptist declared that this is He who I said is preferred before me. In this context John who baptized Jesus and introduced Him into ministry, did it ever so gladly, rejoicing in the fact that the man he just baptized was suppose to be greater than him. He so honored the principle and was not ashamed to declare that Christ was more preferred and greater then He, whose shoelaces he was not worthy to even touch. I must decrease, He must increase. It takes the dying of real mentors to raise the life of future leaders into prominence.

In John 3:28-29 he continues to say, you yourself bear witness that I am not the Christ, but was sent before Him. Every coach, mentor, leader and visionary is sent ahead of those to helped prepare the way and pave their pathway into greatness.

A true mentor protects the birth canal for the bright stars of the future to be born without breach. Greatness releases in love, but myopic thinking prevents the authentic blossoming of seed.

John the Baptist concludes by saying, I am just glad to be a friend of the Bridegroom as he saw the crowd and popular attention shift to Christ. The greatness of John is thereby revealed honorably because he enjoyed the transfer of social favor from him to Christ, who was to pass through his hands into prominence. It is therefore stated that of all born of women, there is no greater prophet than he in the Old Testament. What a legacy!

Consider this, the baby King Herod tried to kill was the same person John the Baptist honored and inaugurated. Certainly John was greater than Herod. The synopsis of King Herod's leadership versus John's leadership brings two parallel principles which will never meet. You are either a product of one or the other. Don't be a Herodian dream killer. Be a baptizer of greatness releasing leaders into their purpose with joy. Eternity will forever put the wise men who traveled over a thousand miles to celebrate the baby and John the Baptist who set Jesus into His place in the same category. I therefore conclude that wisdom and the baptism of the great, go hand in hand. I pray you are cut from the cloth of wisdom and greatness in the sight of God and man. It looks like the Herodian spirit which pursued the kingly seed (Jesus) to Egypt in futility continued its hunger after the kingly seed of Christ went after John who introduced Jesus into His purpose many years later. How many times in life have great leaders taken the pain for their prodigies? Despite this possibility, John still finished his assignment by protecting and preserving the baptism of the greatest King ever known. Vision worth living for, is sometimes worth dying for. John chose to decrease with his life in order to protect what had to increase, for the benefit of all creation. The head of John the Baptist on a platter was the metaphor of excellence through suffering and greatness through bravery. Let all mentors make the crooked paths straight for the next generation of trailblazers. Generals protect the stature of the army.

The good news is that the death of Jesus on the cross canceled and rooted out permanently the dream-killing dynasty of Herodian wickedness. Although we see the appearance of the sword of the same spirit of Herod in Acts chapter 12, it was blocked in verse 5 by the prayer of the saints which provoked to send the angel to Peter setting him free and destroying Herod in verse 23. By the conclusive victory of the cross, the enemy tries to bring shadows of the past but the prevailing prayers of the righteous, in our journey of purpose, are always rewarded by the swift assistance of heaven. We are in partnership with heaven to silence anything that is contrary to the purpose of God.

> *Blotting out the handwriting of ordinances that was against us, which was contrary to us, and took it out of the way, nailing it to his cross; And having spoiled principalities and powers, he made a shew of them openly, triumphing over them in it.* **Colossians 2:14-15**

He that the son has set free is free indeed. The seed of Godly kingship today is lifted far above the dream killing dynasty of darkness. It was finished on the cross by the Author and the Finisher of our faith. Your purpose is free to flourish indeed! Every person called of God today on the journey of *the power of one* is free to finish their course without the Herodian threat. We can do all things through Christ that strengthens us.

A CHOSEN VESSEL

In the wake of Ananias' (Apostle of Damascus) objection to the choice of God, the Lord overruled all the natural logical reasons why Paul should not become a member of Christian leadership in their time. The Lord told him that he (Paul) is a chosen vessel. The choice of God is based on unnatural, illogical, inhuman and unpractical tendencies. It is not a subject of human discussion, but of the sovereign mandate of the Most High, Creator and Governor of heaven and earth, the Commander in Chief of the God-kind and the determinant of purpose, in eternity and time, visible and invisible. He makes His move on people without the permission of any creature. He is God, who therefore imposes His sovereign plan, objective and decisive to use whom He wants, when and how, according to the results He intends to produce without fail. It is this reason why vessels are designed to perfection, in order to meet the results expected. For instance the very height, the bone structure, the mental thinking processes of a person is deliberately established by God because of how He wants to use them; so nothing is a mistake in God concerning you. Rejoice in who you are because you are to meet a need that will surely bring a smile to God! You are made in His image and after His likeness to the intent that He takes the glory. The glory is automatically His and absolutely so.

LEFT ALONE

The subject of Jacob cannot be ignored; It is a typeset of impact before results. In Genesis 32:24-32 it is recorded that Jacob was left alone. Consider the attribute of God to set things up before they happen which is literally an unbeatable hallmark of His excellence. Knowing all things from the beginning to the end, derives the exact intended result, calculated to fit His eternal plan and purpose. In Genesis 32:24 the Bible states:

- And Jacob was left alone
- And there wrestled a man with him unto the breaking of day

It is of a great importance for every individual vessel used by God to enjoy moments of learning to be alone in God's atmosphere and presence. Being alone and being left alone can sometimes become the most productive moments of your life. In most cases, as much it may seem like circumstances put that season into demand, there is always the truth of God's hand deliberately setting it all up providentially, because of the mega derivatives, heaven enjoys to draw from it. There is no sovereign master plan like God's. He makes all things beautiful in His time. Jacob yielded to being alone under the pressure of that time. He was in a non-fighting mode for self-defense because of the brokenness and the phobia of meeting Esau. God found him very vulnerable naturally, but extremely ready spiritually, for a life-changing encounter initiated by God to produce godly results.

> *And Jacob was left alone; and there wrestled a man with him until the breaking of the day. And when he saw that he prevailed not against him, he touched the hollow of his thigh; and the hollow of Jacob's thigh was out of joint, as he wrestled with him. And he said, Let me go, for the day breaketh. And he said, I will not let thee go, except thou bless me. And he said unto him, What is thy name? And he said, Jacob. And he said, Thy name shall be called no more Jacob, but Israel: for as a prince hast thou power with God and with men, and hast prevailed. And Jacob asked him, and said, Tell me, I pray thee, thy name. And he said, Wherefore is it that thou dost ask after my name? And he blessed him there. And Jacob called the name of the place Peniel: for I have seen God face to face, and my life is preserved. And as he passed over Peniel the sun rose upon him, and he halted upon his thigh.*
>
> *Therefore the children of Israel eat not of the sinew which shrank, which is upon the hollow of the thigh, unto this day because he touched the hollow of Jacob's thigh in the sinew that shrank.*
>
> **Genesis 32:24-32**

225

An angel came from heaven to wrestle with him. Note, it wasn't Jacob who initiated the encounter. It was God who started the fight and eventually broke the hollow of his thigh leaving an indelible mark as sign and a memorial on the physical body of the patriarch. This kind of encounter from God which changed Saul to Paul in the New Testament also transformed Jacob to Israel in the birthing of the name and great nation today. Jacob saw God not because he wanted to see Him, but because God came to meet Him. In the scenario of Abraham we see a similar format of God coming to meet Abraham and presenting to him His term of reference:

> *And I will make of thee a great nation, and I will bless thee, and make thy name great; and thou shalt be a blessing: And I will bless them that bless thee, and curse him that curseth thee: and in thee shall all families of the earth be blessed.* **Genesis 12:2-3**

This visitation from the Most High God produced out of Abraham the tribe of the Hebrews, but for Jacob, the people of Israel. The Hebrews came out of the loins of Abraham to produce Isaac, Esau and Jacob; a tribe of people who knew of God and saw His ways in the most unbelievable dimensions of untold grace in the Old Testament. However, the birthing of Israel brought upon the Hebrews a new inspiration of intimacy from God. So the Hebrews were on one level but the name Israel brought them to the next level in God. All this was by the divine plan of God with Abraham and Jacob who having no clue and having never prayed about it, found themselves walking the pathways of God into things that were already predetermined to happen to them. All this in specific prophetic timings brought much glory to God.

Being left alone in God's presence is always very incubational with fresh values, deeper purposes and understandings. God always desires the we spend time with Him, and be alone with Him so we can grow in Him, defining our purpose in God's presence. As much as it is the perfect design of God, it is His most passionate delight for vessels in His hand to desire the same.

King David said, "As the deer pants for the water, so pants my soul for You, O God." The truth is, if I may humbly say, that it is the same song that God sings to His beloved, "As a deer pants for the water brook so HIS soul longs for us; *and Jacob was left alone.* At that moment in time only God knows how much of the emotions of Jacob stirred His passion to hear God, to see God because of the crossroads in view in his life. God was sensitive to His own divine timing, knowing the exact moment in time Jacob was to receive the encounter of the Most High and zeroed in of the birthing of the great nation according to His promises, this time not in words or in type but with a definite name and identity.

For as said by the angel who encountered Jacob in Genesis 32:28, "You have wrestled with God and man and you have prevailed, a prince therefore shall thou become." It is therefore the *princely manifestation* of the seven "I wills" of God given to Abraham in Genesis 12:2-3:

- I will make thee a great nation
- I will bless thee
- I will make that name great
- Thou shall be a blessing
- I will bless them that bless thee
- I will curse them that curse thee
- In thee shall all the families of the earth be blessed

This being said, the prophetic word of God's purpose upon Abraham set Jacob up as the chosen patriarch to be wrestled by God for a definitive name. The content of what it meant for Israel to be a prince, was revealed in the seven "I wills" of God. *What a great nation and what a great name derived out of ONE man in a lonely place!* What great productivity came out of God's impact on Jacob! Birthing a generation of people (biologically and prophetically) and creating a nation whose capital today is Jerusalem; also to become the name of the new heaven and the new earth, according to His promise.

- May your encounters with God produce the utmost deep desires in the heart of God.
- May you never underestimate the wholeness of the glory, the power and the creative skills of God through you.
- You are the one!

They that wait upon the Lord shall definitely renew their strength and identity. In your lonely waiting with prayer and meditation, you will mount up with wings as eagles. This is the reason why you will always run and not be weary, and you will walk and never faint. This is as a result of the nature of His divine impact upon you. Since God is a Spirit and spirits never get weary and tired, we partake of that divine nature. Learn to enjoy being alone with God as the one man, chosen by Him and designed to walk in power for results.

The Apostle Paul writes to Timothy as a second generation seed of the impact, as one of the young men imparted by the impacts received from Christ. Paul emphasized to him that the obedience of one man in the hand of God can set the stage for the many generations to emulate and follow after.

> *Howbeit for this cause I obtained mercy, that in me*
> *first Jesus Christ might shew forth all longsuffering,*
> *for a pattern to them which should hereafter believe*
> *on him to life everlasting.* **I Timothy 1:16**

Your calling does not end with you; it is the beginning of other people's journey being birthed through you.

It is imperative for us to therefore wage a good warfare and protect our prophecy by not yielding to the perspective schemes of darkness. Their daily desire is to trip the righteous from their pathways of glory. May you always contend for your faith, purpose, destiny, dignity and your anointing in the sight of God. He speaks further to Timothy counseling him:

> *Take heed unto thyself, and unto the doctrine;*
> *continue in them: for in doing this thou shalt both*

save thyself, and them that hear thee.

I Timothy 4:16

It is important for every singular person in the hand of God to build a culture of protecting your union with God through the understanding only your mandate can give you. Please, preserve your salvation with fear and trembling for it is your due diligence to do so. The power of one man in the hand of God is a subject for all men who desire to succeed according to the will of God. Therefore be grateful that God enjoys you being left alone where He can become your singular audience. Every encounter with Him makes you stronger and more fit for the assignment laid before you.

Jacob the patriarch became Jacob the prophet whose name was changed to Israel. The birthing of the nation and its name came out of an encounter with the Lord, which consequently shifted the direction and the status of the people of Israel before God, into the prophetic. The extent that it can be said that the transformation of Jacob to Israel was as it were that he was "born again" due to the transformation that usually follows after being in the presence of the Lord as one man who finds his position in the sphere of the most High God.

In Luke 10:39-42, Jesus the tangible presence of the Most High God, comes into the house of Mary and Martha. As Mary sat at His feet receiving the word, Martha was busy with the logical necessities of life. Questioning the reason why Christ would entertain that, Jesus said Mary had chosen the good part by sitting alone in His presence, which shall not be taken away from her. The journey to greatness is through finding your place alone in God. It's in discovering for yourself what you were born for, according to the predetermined counsel of the Lord. "Be you" is often said, but can only be possible when you let God make you who He made you to be through consistency and a developed lifestyle of patiently longing after his counsel, presence, glory and will. In Psalm 63:1-8 King David said, "My soul follows hard after Thee to see Thy power and thy glory." The destinies of the great and mighty born of God have always come to pass and conclusively brings smiles into the very heart of God, because of the desire to be in tune with the original blueprint of God for one's own life.

> *Sacrifice and offering thou did not desire; mine ears hast thou opened: burnt offering and sin offering hast thou not required. Then said I, Lo, I come: in the volume of the book it is written of me, I delight to do thy will, O my God: yea, thy law is within my heart.* **Psalm 40:6-8**

In Psalm 40 David declares that his life on this earth is to replay that which is written in the book of God in eternity. He says, "I delight to do thy will." There is no way you can enjoy being alone with God unless you have a great delight to do His will. The measure to which you desire to do his will is the measure to which you will fulfill His will. Progress and prosperity does not please God except that it manifests the reason for which you were created.

In Genesis 45:8 Joseph had been sold by his brothers away into destruction and after many years introduces himself to them as the prime minister of Egypt - the most powerful nation on the earth at the time. Since it is known that civilization began out of Egypt, he was then the governor of the most civilized world of his time. This one man in the hand of God was processed through pain but came out as pure and polished gold, making the incredible statement that, "*God has made me a father to pharaoh, lord of all his house, and a ruler throughout all the land of Egypt.*"

Greatness without God is like building a mansion on sand. But with God it is like building an advanced city on the eternal rock of ages. May your delight always be found in being alone in God's presence, as consistently as you may. It is not your desire that makes it possible, but it is rather the demands of the eternal plan of God for your life that determine this requirement. Lay hold of the vision from God and you will desire to be with Him to see its absolute fulfillment and manifestation. May God be your role model as He relates to you and brings you up from levels of weakness to strength and strength to greater strength and even to excellence. You are the one person in the hand of a great God who made you in His image and after His likeness that you may have dominion over all the works of His hands.

CHAPTER 22:

THE WITNESS OF TWO

In his great making, the Apostle Paul had an extraordinary experience with the Lord. None of his lieutenants who journeyed with him that day saw not the Lord, but he himself.

> *And the men which journeyed with him stood speechless, hearing a voice, but seeing no man. And Saul arose from the earth; and when his eyes were opened, he saw no man: but they led him by the hand, and brought him into Damascus. And he was three days without sight, and neither did eat nor drink.* **Acts 9:7-9**

Every one man called by God must be raised by God through the processes predetermined according to the will of God. As important as the process is, so is the event. A *witness* is carved out of your personal experience which only you and God can talk about with understanding. No one else is able to comprehend what you have gone through, what you are going through, and what your purpose is all about. God always establishes deep a witness in your inner spirit that lets you know, that you know that you know what is required of you. Every single person who dares to walk the path with God, will walk through the path of *the witness of two*. That's when you know that you know, that God knows, that you know, what He made you to become! Lay hold of this experience; let no one take it away from you. To a large extent even the enemy cannot talk you out of it nor dissuade you unless by choice you decide to dishonor God and backslide. Moses was with the Lord forty days and forty nights.

> *And he was there with the LORD forty days and forty nights; he did neither eat bread, nor drink water. And he wrote upon the tables the words of the covenant, the ten commandments. And it came to pass, when Moses came down from mount Sinai with the two tables of testimony in Moses' hand, when he came down from the mount, that Moses wist not that the skin of his face shone while he talked with him. And when Aaron and all the*

children of Israel saw Moses, behold, the skin of his
face shone; and they were afraid to come nigh him.

Exodus 34:28:30

And this incredible testimony of God encountering a man in the seclusion of exclusivity, in His amazing presence on Mount Sinai for forty days and forty nights without food and water; there are no other witnesses beside Moses and the Lord that can tell the story of their communion together. The depths of your walk with God become so passionately personal as deep calls unto deep, leaving the experience too deep to express to a third party; *the witness of two.* It is a pathway the mighty; the movers and shakers are required to walk through. It is not a path for anyone to experience for you, only you yourself. This experience sets you apart and distinguishes you from every other person in your generation. Exodus 33:14-16 is a case in point where the Lord said, "My presence shall go with you and I will give you rest."

The nation that was born out of wrestling with God received the name *Israel* in God's presence. The 'Law of Beginnings' certainly applied in this case which says that which was from the beginning sets the precedent for the rest of the journey. Born of God's presence, they grew in God's presence and were to thrive in God's presence. However, in the great scene of worshiping the golden calf, the Lord chose to leave them alone since they called the golden idol their god ultimately inferring that they were disowning God to follow another. In Moses' intercession and pleading for mercy and restoration, Moses said to God that, "If Thy presence will not go *with me, the leader,* then take us *corporately* no further, for it is by this encounter of Your presence daily that we are separate and distinguished from all the other people of the earth."

Certainly proving that by the witness of two, God and Israel, could not be understood by any other nation of the earth because of the depth of experience in the Lord, His glory, His passion, His love, His power, and His nature. The nation of Israel, their fathers, their patriarchs, and generations have the witness of two recorded of God and His people to the extent that He is called, 'the God of Israel' and Israel is called 'the Israel of God.' May you enjoy such accolade of God literally owning you and bringing you into such fellowship where you share a similar ownership in return; the witness of two. When two agree on anything on this earth it shall be done!

It is an amazing journey of one ending up with a witness of two; the divine and the natural; the super and the natural; ; producing outlandish productivity and results with breakthroughs never before told. Such a close knit walk with God becomes the breeding ground for the trailblazing of great inventions, ideas, dreams, and fulfillments never to be repeated or duplicated; the witness of two. May you lay hold on this amazing journey between you and God. The witness of two is the breakthrough with God.

The experiences enjoyed by the witness of two are priceless. They strengthen your resolve and stabilize your direction. It leaves in you the unshakable belief systems that make you survive challenges, tragedies and triumphs of your journey. They lead you on the narrow path of God's highway with the words, "My ways are high, so are My thoughts." The experience of *the witness of two*_brings you into such a high life of contentment. The external troubles and turbulences, which may be outwardly visible, will be as the peace of the still waters echoing the voice of the Lord, daily saying to you, "Be still and know that I am God; *the witness of two.*"

In Matthew 14, when Peter walked on the water with Jesus, that experience could only be enjoyed and understood by the witness of two, Jesus and Peter. Many years later, possibly in heaven as they chat, no one else can understand the experience in that moment in time walking on water but he and Jesus. It will always be that insightful inspiration of the two witnesses that sets them apart from the ordinary thinking formula of mankind. Lay hold of your witness with God because He will not let you go until He has fulfilled the purpose for which He called you.

In Genesis 28:11-15, Jacob had a dream under open heavens experience he had from God, the Lord said, I will not let you go until I have done that which I have spoken of thee, I will not let you go." In this witness of the two, there was developed an intimacy of possessiveness between God and Jacob. The understanding that is developed in such intimacy of the two increases as they continue to invest loyalty, experience, cohesion and priceless value in their emotions and passions for each other. Jacob held on to that confidence of what he saw of God and knew of God that made a young man holding on to faith unequivocal to any of his day. The Lord was with him as super glue adhesive; *what a bonding of triumph and understanding!* Jacob grew through those experiences and became the patriarch that birthed Israel into being. The witness of two is always a growing experience from glory to glory. So it is on the day of Pentecost in Acts 2:2-5, the scripture states that the Holy Ghost came upon each individual of the 120 people in the upper room, to the extent that each person had their own personal development of *the witness of two*; with the evidence of speaking in the language of God and enjoying the beautiful presence of His glory and power.

There were 120 singular human entities, each having their own witness of two with God directly. Whereas the outside world was wondering what was going on, the inner man was filled with that which only the Holy Spirit could adequately express the depths of such an experience. Yet some mocked saying that they were drunk with new wine, for the witness of two is an experience that is quite intoxicating. This is an experience where leaders get passionate with dreams that drive them as intoxicated people, listening to no one and enjoying nothing more than the activity of the revelation. This wonderful euphoria creates a personal sphere of influence that only you and God enjoy. The presence of the witness of two makes a person oblivious to the outside world of doubts, questions, and negativity.

Just as Peter, walking on the water with Jesus, should not have cared about the storm but just stayed focused and connected to the vision of walking on water; not knowing how much deeper that journey would have taken him. I believe other dimensions of scripture would have been unfolded if he had just stayed focused on walking with Jesus on that water. I'm quite certain many more books would have been written about that journey. It is possible this did not take place nor Peter gone beyond the point of sinking, because he had not yet, at that point received the Holy Ghost, who would have given him the courage and fortitude to prevail over the storm. But now after the day of Pentecost, filled with the experience of the witness of two, we see Peter handling much stormier weather then that stormy sea and he triumphed all the days of his life.

In Acts 1:8, Jesus said, "Ye shall be witnesses unto Me." Oh what an incredible journey of two, and you bear witness to Him individually as a sovereign partner.

The witness of two; an incredible call to walk into a realm that is far more gratifying than the external fruit of achievements we long to see. It is deeper than the harvest because it develops a spirit to Spirit tie with your God. It is an indelible memory and experience which lives forever in eternity. Moments where you lock your eyes with your God in heaven; both of you nodding your heads in understanding of the journey you have experienced in life and will in eternity. This is the kind of experience that can be said, "Only you know." In the very heights and depths of your journey into purpose, there are many who say, "How did you get there? How do you know you have arrived there?" And every person who can attest to this experience, can have only one answer which is, "You will know when you know."

It is an unusual kind of favor that God would call a people or an individual for such a journey of the *power of one;* becoming the witness of two. If for any reason you lost your pattern, may mercy find you and restore you. May the mercy seat of God recall your name again and re-enlist you because that's who He is; the God of all mercy. But if you are already on this journey, may grace abound to you, grace upon grace. This is an incredible walk of God's grace.

Grace therefore, is the condescending (coming down) of the Most High God to the level of mortal, weak and frail man so as to lift him to the realm of the *God-tribe* in stature, in wisdom with the manifestation of outstanding results. As Titus declares, the grace of God has appeared to all men, therefore all men are qualified to stay strong in this journey, but the decision is left to the individual to make. May your choices feed your journey positively.

The witness of two has been the one key reason of success according to the standard of God achievable by anyone, anytime, and anywhere. The truth and the fact that He is omnipotent makes Him omniscient and therefore omnipresent. This is relevantly why no one on this earth can feel left out or with an excuse. God can be with the Eskimo fulfilling the witness of two as well as with the Australian making great strides. The witness of two is why King David succeeded and declared boldly:

For thou wilt light my candle: the Lord my God will enlighten my darkness. For by thee I have run through a troop; and by my God have I leaped over a wall. As for God, His way is perfect. The word of the Lord is tried. He is a buckler to all those that trust in him. For who is God save the Lord? Or who is a rock save our God? It is God that girdeth me with strength, and maketh my way perfect. He maketh my feet like hinds' feet, and setteth me upon my high places. **Psalm 18:28-33**

In David's definition of the witness of two, he explains it as the hind runs at a certain velocity, being the most sure-footed animal in the heights of mountainous terrain, the deer's feet land at the same spot of the front legs creating the footprints of two and not four. David therefore was saying that as, "I have walked with God, I have to follow Him footprint by footprint, step by step, and because my footprints yearn to step into His footprints, what you see is two footprints instead of four. The hind feet of the deer are used to show intimate fellowship with God to the extent that His footprints become my stepping stones; as I step into God's "hot spots" which are always found in the highest places of elevation and glory.

Anyone who can be like the hinds' feet of the deer in God and to God, enjoys the levels and the passionate grace of divine exploits. May you always connect to your high places by stepping exactly into the perfect will of God for your life which is always found in the highways of the Most High; the witness of two. Melchizedek pronounced a blessing on Abraham in Genesis 14:19 calling him, Abraham of the Most High, possessor of the heaven and the earth.

We being filled with the Holy Spirit, according to Acts 2, are connected to the *hinds' feet of the deer* principle by walking in symphony with God, making melodies, speaking His oracles, and fulfilling great results beyond human capacity. The apostles became so one with God through the Holy Ghost that in Acts 15:28 they could make statements like, "For it seemed good to the Holy Ghost, and to us…" The witness of two culminating in Thessalonica in Acts 17:6, "For these that have turned the world upside down have come hither also."

Oh how wonderful and how glorious is it for ordinary man to fit so much into God's perfect will as it said "it fits like a glove" to share the same pathways, cultures, vision, and rhythm with the Most High for fulfillment. May God bless and make you strong in the witness of two. Paul said in Acts 17:28, "For in Him we live and move and have our being."

In Acts 27:14-25, being tormented by the tempestuous wind called the Euroclydon, Paul speaks to the captain of the boat in which they were sailing to Rome and said, "Fear not for there stood by me this night the angel of God whose I am and whom I serve." The witness of two is the greatest testimony any man can hold on to, calling himself a personal possession of God and also declaring himself to be an intimate servant of Jehovah. This is the greatest accolade angels can witness of you. The witness of two is a major faith dynamic pathway, proclaiming the synergy between the person of God and the person of man. You learn to know and experience the Trinity of God on personal turfs, then you can say as Paul said, "For I believe God that it shall be as it was told me." Your journey with God in the fulfillment of high purpose creates in you such strength of faith and immovable understanding of His ability, capacity, and creativity to do all things. You don't just confirm what is written in the scriptures of God, but your experiences in Him confirm the unshakable truthfulness of His counsel in all matters.

A true believer in God is what you become when He picks you as one singular person and transforms you into the pathway of the witness of two. There is a plain field you attain in God through faith, where He makes Himself known to you as well you make yourself known to Him. It is the kind of picture where you shift from serving God into friendship with God. It is then that He can say, "I know you."

> *And the LORD said, Shall I hide from Abraham that thing which I do; Seeing that Abraham shall surely become a great and mighty nation, and all the nations of the earth shall be blessed in him? For I know him, that he will command his children and his household after him, and they shall keep the way of the LORD, to do justice and judgment; that the LORD may bring upon Abraham that which he hath spoken of him.* **Genesis 18:17-19**

In the journey of the power of one, there is a development behind the scenes of a continuous one-on-one fellowship where the secrets of God are revealed to those that fear Him. Atmospheres like this put your heart on God's microscope where He can trust you absolutely. It is the journey of the absolute man and the absolute God fulfilling absolute mandates of greatness in the land of the living.

CHAPTER 23:

FAITH READINESS

The essential motivation for every person living on earth is the hope to achieve purpose, fulfillment and a good destiny. Hope is an essential life-giving aspiration. It is often said, "keep hope alive," but for this to happen faith is necessary. Faith is defined as the substance of things hoped for and the evidence of things not seen. It is imperative is to understand that faith is the servant of hope which gives substance to things not yet manifested.

Faith is that one thing that God desires to see in the earth according to Luke 18:8, "When the Son of man cometh, shall he find faith on the earth?" This clearly shows that God wants to see faith when he looks on the community of men. It's not our intelligence, brilliance and accomplishments, but faith in Him, His word, His will, His ways, His covenant laws, His principles and His attributes. Fulfilling this incredible divine policy of the faith subject is the reason why God fills His word with His faith and power. As many as receive the inspiration of His unadulterated word, faith is born in them. Shall God find faith in your house, in your business, in your office, in your prayer closet, meditations, contemplations and decisions? It is what He is looking for. Shall He find faith in the North Pole, in the Americas, New Zealand, what about Asia, Russia, Western and Eastern Europe, around the equator, the tropic of cancer and the tropic of Capricorn, longitude to longitude, from one degree of the earth to the next, shall He find faith? It is a proclamation that requires a mandatory response from everybody in whose nostrils there is breath.

> *Faith is what we receive by connecting to God through His Holy Spirit and from those who are God-centered but believing is what we do in response to His endowment of gracious faith.*

It is the one cardinal attribute that pleases God in every individual that He works and walks with. It is the substance of hope and the graphic evidence of things not yet seen. It's given such strength and drive to as many as dare to trust in the invisible yet incredible God whose ways are more tangible than the flesh next to you. Jehovah is His name. Without faith no one can please or praise Him. He always creates the atmosphere around His faithful, making faith always a part of His people. No matter how wealthy or successful you are, there is always something God will cause you to have faith for. That is His stake in the partnership of purpose. You MUST have faith because He is full of faith. The fact alone that He chose you from a background of defeat and hopelessness to trust into your hands such grandeur grace of success and prominence, is tangible proof of Him exercising His faith in your life. He invested His faith by calling you as one man. He therefore He demands faith from you as a response, to the intent that the witness of two shall have no shipwreck or failure.

Abraham did not stagger in his belief, but was in full persuasion that He who had promised shall not fail. Faith is the evidence of your resolve to "let go and let God." It has often been said that people lose their faith in their journey of following God in His highways. For this to happen though, one must lose their first love in order to lose their faith in Him. The scriptures have confirmed that faith worketh by love (Galatians 5:6). In other words you have to love your call and enjoy your mandate for faith to keep burning as eternal flames of fire in your spirit before God. I pray that you will always keep your love for God and your calling alive and strong. Whatever you can do to protect the purity of your love and vision is your prerogative, but staying connected to great relationships and great dreamers will help keep your faith alive.

Hebrews 11:2 declares that, "By faith the elders obtained a good report," therefore the true character of the nature of faith

247

is that it is a good report producer in the life of all who are called by His name. In the process of God, making you as the hinds' feet of the deer in His presence, your faith in believing and fulfilling what He tells you makes you shine in His countenance as a man who believed unto the end. Faith gives you a good report as you finish your course. Paul said, "I have run the race; I have fought the good fight; I have kept the faith." In other words, I know and I have faith that a crown awaits me in heaven and to all those who believe in His appearing. King David said, "By my God I have run through a troop and leapt over a wall" for his faith in God gave him a good report. Gideon implemented every instruction he received from the angel and restored the glory to Israel. In that final onslaught there were shouts and screams of the sword of the Lord and the sword of Gideon (Judges 7:20-25), in perfect affirmation of the power that is ignited in the witness of two. Faith. Faith. Faith!

THE DUET OF TWO

Jesus Christ, our superior partner in time and eternity is also the Author and Finisher of your faith in God. God the Father deliberately gave us His Son as a bridge that closed the gap created by sin. This synergy is an incredible partnership between God and man. Such a connection inspires the right imagination and vision of excellence and perfection through His Holy Spirit; *the power of two!*

Christ our eternal partner came to our level and did not despise the process because of the vision. Consequently He set a precept of lifting us up to His level. This grace is key to the power of two. Since we can't get to commanding heights on our own, grace came to us. Since we couldn't go up, He came down. God gave Him a name above all names and anointed Him above all else; the most anointed Christ. This is essential for our successful journey.

> *For we are His workmanship created in Christ Jesus*
> *unto good works, which God hath before ordained,*
> *that we should walk in them.* **Ephesians 2:10**

As a father walks his daughter down the aisle to the marriage altar, so Christ also walks the aisle of purpose with every individual person in His Kingdom. The Power of two is a spiritual agreement that discards the mundane, temporary treasures of life. Not putting confidence in the flesh is to shift from a logic drive to a spirit drive, to attain the mark.

> *For we are the circumcision which worship God in*
> *the spirit and rejoice in Christ Jesus and have no*
> *confidence in the flesh.* **Philippians 3:3**

> *Brethren, I count not myself to have apprehended:*
> *but this one thing I do, forgetting those things which*
> *are behind, and reaching forth unto those things*
> *which are before. I press toward the mark for the*
> *prize of the high calling of God in Christ Jesus.*
>
> **Philippians 3:13-14**

There is much weight to offload in the issues of the flesh, in order to attain the spiritual heights of glory. Living out of your flesh modem is stepping out of the box, like Peter who stepped out of the boat to walk on water. The power of two is experienced right there with Christ's invitation for Peter to walk on water. Every single leader of purpose receives an invitation to step out of their boat of natural logic and step into the water mass of spiritual heights of glory. The usual for the unusual. The logical to the illogical. *The power of two* creates this kind of dimensional breakthrough. May you locate the footprints of the Lord and step right into them. Get engaged with *the power of two*. It is the unprecedented fellowship between you and God with one vision and one mission.

THE WITNESS OF TWO

The extra-ordinary principle in *the witness of two* sets the stage for the incredible manifest interplay of the duet of destiny, born of the union of God and man, on the stage of purpose. *The duet of two* is the echo of the witness of two. As a result of one person called of God, the response dares us to lean not on our own understanding, but in all our ways acknowledging God and His expectation for our life. *The duet of two in the sphere of the witness of two.*

God is nurturing and full of faith, meaning that He is faithful in all His ways. Whenever and wherever His presence is allowed to dominate it releases His glory, His light, His weight and grandeur. These also become the very origins of our faith and confidence in Him. Those who walk in God's presence enjoy the endowment of the gift of faith so as to produce the awesome fruit through faith. The journey of one in God is that which inspires supernatural faith, because of the supernatural results to be seen in expectation of the days to come. It behooves us all not to walk by sight, but by faith (2 Cor. 5:7).

The natural elements of life are far below the existing world of the invisible God and His environments. The mystery of walking with such a successful God in the time of limitations and dislocated logic requires advisedly the walk by inspiration, discerning our way in God and trusting Him beyond the logical rhythms. To subject God to logical conclusions is to limit Him to the levels of fleshly decadence. If He calls you, believe Him and if He sends you, obey Him and if He changes your course of direction, love him and love it all. You will be fine. The Shunammite woman saw the great acts of God through Elisha and in spite of the vivid evidence of a dead son in her arms, yet proclaims, "It is well." (2 Kings 4:21-26) I pray your vivid journey with God shall create the symphony for heaven and earth that enunciates the very inspiration that "it is well." For it is spoke of Jesus in Mark 7:37 that he has done all things well and in verses 31-36 by his fingers and the touch of the spit of his tongue the deaf and the speech-impeded person was made whole instantly; a truth that beats logic and stirs up faith as an instrument that establishes the wellness of all things through faith. As you walk through your path of purpose, you are journeying through the ways that demand intentional faith. Your conclusion shall be perfectly well in spite of the odds and the failure syndrome of the may-sayers and nay-sayers. It is well.

The scenario of Hebrews 11:4 reveals two individuals created in the image and likeness of God having the same opportunity with the same aim, goal and aspiration, yet differed by their act of faith. Abel provided his sacrifice by faith and not by sight and excelled in the sight of the Lord.

> *By faith Abel offered unto God a more excellent sacrifice than Cain, by which he obtained witness that he was righteous, God testifying of his gifts and by it he being dead yet speaketh.* **Hebrews 11:4**

One of the main opposing factors of faith, is the strength derived from the logic of sight and sound. Those who move and act by sight, feelings and logic defuse their strength of excellence before the Lord. In other words the weight of your ways before God is much heavier and more valuable when it is done through faith and not by sight. Cain saw the logic of giving God the best of His produce knowing very well that God wasn't going to physically eat of the sacrifice, so he was enticed to devalue his presentation. By doing so he took God's principle for granted. Abel on the other hand would not consider whether it was a naturally wise thing to do or not but gave God the best by faith and did not second-guess the outcome. Abel established a memorial in the heart of God. He being dead yet the impact of his faith giving continued to speak in the heart of God. Faith is the platform for the emergence of greatness, but sight is the devaluation of greatness.

Move by faith and not by sight. It has often been said, "Be careful not to walk in blind faith," but truthfully you can't walk by faith with your eyes open. You have to be truly blind to the 'world of natural reasoning' so as to be open to God's invisible world of power to perform outstandingly; for without faith it is impossible to please Him, and he that comes to God must believe that He is, and that He is a rewarder of those that diligently seek Him (Hebrews 11:6).

DILIGENCE

The principle of the power of one, requires a consistency of diligence towards the desired goal. Diligence is required to prevail in faith. Faith is an unending journey until it serves you with the hope you desire according to the purpose of God for your life. Diligence has no time for laziness. It is said that tough times don't last, but tough people do. If that's true then the lazy do not endure but the diligent do. May you be faith energized, faith-consumed and faith-advanced in your journey from beginning to end. May you grow in faith and in grace as you increase the works of God in your life to the glory of His name. Be blessed in faith and diligence and believe in Christ the King, our Lord and Savior.

2 Corinthians 14:13 declares that, "May the grace of the Lord Jesus Christ, and the love of God, and the communion of the Holy Ghost, be with you all. The breakdown of the individual nature of the triune God shows the Father's instinct of

love and the Lord Jesus Christ's instinct of grace. It also reveals the fellowship and communion instincts of the Holy Spirit that encapsulates whoever finds their place in their midst for great works. I therefore dare to say that your intimacy on this journey of the power of one strengthens you in loving God with understanding as well as understanding the grace with which Christ made you a new creation, while at the same time the Holy Spirit embraces you in an intimate common-union and fellowship in the unimaginable dimension of association. This three-fold daily encounter with God makes you the fourth person in the midst of the three-person-lifestyle of the divine "First Family". Your human spirit is designed to handle this incredible divine overflow of the trinity. Therefore, fear not the journey with God. Just trust and believe that He is calling you into the pathway with Him for which you were created. You can handle this! Enjoying the love of God and participating in the grace of the Lord makes you appreciate fellowship with the Holy Spirit. Through the grace of our Lord Jesus Christ you are able to encapsulate understanding love and all its power and mystery of an amazing journey of fellowship and friendship with the Holy Spirit who is our Comforter, our Helper, Teacher, Counselor and our Paraclete.

CHAPTER 24:

THE PRAYER FACTOR

Prayer is one of God's most trusted spiritual technologies given to man to work with. It is established to keep the synergy between heaven and earth without fail. It is the channel of fellowship, worship, connectivity, strength, affirmation, productivity, heritage and belonging. Created to work together as a network, heaven was made first, then the earth. It is one of the keys of the Kingdom of God that opens the heavens to access all that He is and all that He has and all we need.

> *In the beginning God created the heaven and the earth.*
> **Genesis 1:1**

This scripture means the earth came out of heaven and is therefore to function perfectly with the same policies and principles that made God's dwelling place blissful and eternally glorious. The union between heaven and earth caused our planet to be mostly on the receiving end of God's glory, power, beauty and total governance in partnership with man. In other cases the needs of heaven are fulfilled on earth as God desires. The permanent residence of the Most High God in heaven graciously made this earth to be a heaven on earth experience as exemplified in the creation of the Garden of Eden. By this I mean, if Adam had not fallen, I suppose God may have expanded the garden to cover the whole earth as man's population increased. Eden therefore was the prototype of what was to come for the planet; a beautiful masterpiece designed to be the example of the ultimate earth.

However this dwelling place of humanity is to stay tuned to heaven's demands, desires, plans, influence and purpose. Every good and perfect gift needed to advance the potentials of mankind is to be released from the Father of lights, in whom there is no variableness nor shadow of turning. Such an inseparable partnership of an excellent working venture was to determine the rulership of all creation and its fulfillment. Man was placed in charge of this side of creation, *the earth* and its government by the dominion mandate given.

The heaven, even the heavens, are the Lord's: but the earth hath he given to the children of men.

Psalm 115:16

The fall of man through deception robbed the first leaders of earth their duty and dominion mandate. Adam gave away his authority by choice, because he did not follow through with God's instructions. In Luke 4:5-7, the devil said to Jesus that the power of the earth had been delivered to Him, therefore justifying why He could exercise such authority, by doing what he wanted at will. The fall of Lucifer dropped him to a lower state of being; the lowest ever known to eternity and time, but by Adam's disobedience he exchanged places with Satan's fallen state. In other words, Adam allowed the enemy to have what was given in to him in the garden. Satan was promoted to Adam's status and Adam was reduce to satan's fallen state. This was an ungodly exchange. This unclean governance over the earth entirely disrupted the original link and partnership between heaven and earth.

THE BEGINNING OF PRAYER

We find out in Genesis 4:26 that from the days of Seth, men began to call upon the name of the Lord. The third son of Adam and Eve may have possibly received a comprehension of where his parents had fallen from, what they lost, and what needs to be gained back. This provoked in him, the passion and crave for God's intervention. Men began to call upon the name of the Lord because of the pain of human dysfunction.

Prayer is the connection between man and God for partnership that leads to restoration, productivity, contentment and fulfillment. This inspiration runs through the entire Bible as to the desire of men prompting a living God of love and grace for help beyond man's ability. The original estate of man was to function far above what we see today. Made in the image and the likeness of God, we were established by heritage to walk in the God-class, which is the next level above the angelic world. Falling far below the angels, established a permanency of groaning, lack, need, pain and oppression for mankind. Prayer is to avert this.

Prayer is therefore, according to the Bible, the subject *for victory* over what was lost. The determination and passion to rule again in God's gracious gift of dominion begin to arise when the righteous begin to get hold of *the need to fulfill purpose* like Seth. Designed to walk in dominion, yet deprived of its tools and the platform to function, created the frustration of the human race. Every generations began to look for alternative means to satisfy the crave to function correctly; thus idol worship began. Idolatry is the subject of serving God in a manner not approved by Him. Adam lost his authority of rulership to the devil, which gave the archenemy of God the privilege to resist man from playing his original role with God. As a result, the devil and his fallen angels found the "middleman role" to use as a strategy to resist connectivity, block access and even cut the link between God and His plans for man. As in Daniel 10:10-14 we see the angelic account of how the prince of Persia, a fallen angel under satanic authorities, resisted the breakthrough of Daniel.

This ungodly interference has made it tough to pray or seek God. It is noticeable that in all the enterprises of man, prayer sometimes is the most difficult because of the menace. Breakthroughs became the hunger of every person who desired the original freedom God created us to have. This strange arrangement due to the fall therefore has required a strong belief system in God to fight for what was lost. But for the persistence of the prophet Daniel in prayer and fasting, the enemy could have succeeded in depriving an Old Testament saint from what was his. The legal powers given to Adam to determine life and prosperity was now in the hands of Satan who dared to utilized that office treacherously, where damage was done to the plans of God for man and his own goodwill towards fellow mankind. Thank God for people who will not accept the devil's pressure or instincts to subject good people to second class or a lesser privileges than ordained by God. Refuse to be robbed and press in for what is yours! In Hebrews 11 it is recorded that by this faith of perseverance, through suffering, they obtained a good report. They travailed by sweat and blood, not allowing the curse of the law to restrict them. They did their best and God was pleased.

THE OLD TESTAMENT EQUATION

The Old Testament shows how men and women had to fight for victory. Prayers required many painful sacrifices if breakthroughs were needed because of the curse of the law. In other words God made curse a law, by His pronouncements on and against the serpent who deceived Eve, and on Eve who influenced Adam to disobey God.

Genesis 3:14-21 shows us that:

• The serpent was cursed to crawl on its belly and to eat

dust all the days of its life.

- God established enmity between the seed and the generation of the serpent which is evil, and the woman and her seed and generation of humanity. Permanent war and hatred was established.
- God multiplied the sorrows of women.
- God calls the ground, which is the earth and its soil, cursed, impacting man and his working days with sorrows, thorns and thistles, so as to create sweat and difficulty in prosperity.

These determinate words of the Most High, comprised what He told Adam, "That the day you shall eat the fruit of this tree, you shall surely die (Genesis 2:17)." This death was the cutting off of the link between God and man which totally removed man from the incredible, glorious synergy with God and His sphere of influence of which man was designed to abide in permanently. Making it simple, God pulled the plug and the lights went out. This was necessary for God to do because if man chose to obey the devil, God would not be party to that friendship. Man chose to go with the devil and deny God. God chose to separate Himself from that network because man did not need Him anymore by implication. God will not cohabit with the devil's influence over man and thus trouble began. The need for prayer became a necessity.

Coming out of those pronouncements turned curses into law. The troubles created by these curses became so heavy that the only way of breaking through into blessing, which would involve God's help, was through pain and sacrifice. These were matters which can only be resolved by blood created by God; hence the need for blood sacrifices to get God's attention. Since blood cries and speaks by its nature, the inception of prayer through sacrifice on altars through the Old Testament, amplified the need of man as connected to that sacrifice. The voice of the sacrifice came into agreement with man's grief and passion for badly needed breakthroughs. Whether in times of thanksgiving, praise or in miracles, blood sacrifices and burnt offerings were the only acceptable frequencies that God would respond to. Because of the curse of the law that out of man's sweat and sorrows shall he eat and have a breakthrough, blood sacrifices communicated sweat, pain and sorrows for an atonement that could be accepted for a moment in time. It was time that people appealed to God for victory through the practice of blood sacrifices.

I Samuel 7:8-9 says that Samuel took a suckling lamb and offered it for a burnt offering holy unto the Lord, and the Lord heard him. Genesis 46:1-7 says that Jacob went to Bersheeba and presented sacrifice on his grandfather's and father's altar to hear a response from God as to whether to go to Egypt. Desiring to see if Joseph was truly alive he presented a sacrifice and heard from God. In I Kings 18:36-39, Elijah got a response from God by burning a sacrifice. As a result, was prayer was synonymous to answers and victory.

*Christ hath redeemed us from the curse of the law,
being made a curse for us: for it is written, Cursed
is every one that hangeth on a tree. That the blessing
of Abraham might come on the Gentiles through
Jesus Christ; that we might receive the promise of
the Spirit through faith.* **Galatians 3:13-14**

The curse of the law was spoken before the covenant was made. The law of the Old Testament was not entirely a curse but was given when the curse had been a law, after God pronounced the curse on Adam and Even in the Garden of Eden. He drove them out and shut down the premises. I can understand why it was shut down, because a curse entered Eden. It could not be allowed to operate with the yeast of rebellion, sin and curse. God was ready for a new thing.

Galatians 3:13 Old Testament Equation = Limitations in prayer.

Galatians 3:14 New Testament Covenant = Limitations lifted off prayer.

THE NEW TESTAMENT PROVISION

The New Testament provision for prayer is a better plan in which He changed the priesthood by sacrificing His own son, on the altar of Calvary once and for all. The bloody death of Jesus on the cross, was the lamb that was slain in the Old Testament days, but this time the Lamb of God. God took His only Son, saw Him and gave Him as a lamb, whose eternal blood would speak permanently on behalf of all for atonement, redemption, restoration, forgiveness, reconciliation and dominion. Forevermore there would be no need for sweat, sorrows and pain for a breakthrough.

> *Jesus, when he had cried again with a loud voice,*
> *yielded up the ghost. And, behold, the veil of the*
> *temple was rent in twain from the top to the bottom;*
> *and the earth did quake, and the rocks rent.*

Matthew 27:50-51

On His cross when He yielded up the ghost on Calvary, the veil in the temple (a good ways away) split from top to bottom. Mankind separated by his sin nature and prayer were both blocked from having easy access to God; this being exemplified by the veil. Separating the temple from the Holy of Holies was this great veil, but because of the price Christ paid, the veil was split or removed.

By this act of God's mercy, the lid was removed from the prayer lifestyle of saints and now through prayer we can have access to the most intimate oracles of the Most High. By His name for as many as believe by faith, the heavens are open to lay hold of the most powerful God, to do the most incredible acts of kindness, anywhere, anytime. While the Old Testament did not have this kind of access, we do. The veil was split from top to bottom so that we could enter into intimate fellowship with the Most High; thereby being able to come right into His presence and right into His throne room to obtain mercy and grace at our time of need. The veil split so we could have access.

Apostle Paul writes to the church of Ephesus:

> *But now in Christ Jesus ye who sometimes were far*
> *off are made nigh by the blood of Christ. For he*
> *is our peace, who hath made both one, and hath*
> *broken down the middle wall of partition between*
> *us; having abolished in his flesh the enmity, even*
> *the law of commandments contained in ordinances;*
> *for to make in himself of twain one new man, so*
> *making peace...* **Ephesians 2:13-15**

Being brought into a reconciled state with our God, in His body which was broken on the cross of Calvary, Jesus dealt away with enmity between us and our Creator. Very essentially He became our peace, who broke down the middle wall of partition between us, abolishing the law of commandments in ordinance, that we could enter into the new. He is our peace. Therefore with confidence we can have peace in God's presence through the mystery of the transactions of His blood on our behalf. We therefore have peaceful access through prayer.

As a result the enemy has limited access to us; the control of satanic influence was destroyed and the ungodly interference, dealt with thoroughly. This being done, every case of accusation that was contrary to the perfect will of God for us is dismissed. We are therefore discharged and acquitted from ungodly allegations and strange and mysterious contracts. Even though the enemy had labels against God's people, in the New Testament provision was made so that every one singular mandate given to an individual, can empower us to run the race of destiny, purpose and leadership to the end. We have peace with God, therefore we can access His power. We have peace in Christ therefore all that He says we are, we are. The middle wall of partition was broken down. The oil of prayer is flowing.

What the Old Testament practiced often, we had done for us one time resulting in a better covenant and results. Therefore it is in the name of Jesus all prayers can be answered if we believe.

> *After this, Jesus knowing that all things were now accomplished, that the scripture might be fulfilled, saith,* **I thirst.** *Now there was set a vessel full of vinegar and they filled a sponge with vinegar, and put it upon hyssop, and put it to his mouth. When Jesus therefore had received the vinegar, he said,* **It is finished** *and he bowed his head, and gave up the ghost.* **In John 19:28-30**

When Jesus, knowing that all things were accomplished, said, "I thirst," the process of His judgment and resurrection was God's way of packaging all the spiritual, physical, and emotional consequences of Adam's error and the devil's dominion into one strategy. God as all wisdom, broke the curse of the law, the devil's authority and rulership, deceptions, diseases, oppression, failures, poverty (physical and spiritual) and bareness. All of these and more were reversed because of the voice of the blood of Jesus that spoke on our behalf.

And to Jesus the mediator of the new covenant,
and to the blood of sprinkling, that speaketh better
things than that of Abel. **Hebrews 12:24**

It is his blood that speaks better things speaks for us today.

He said "I thirst" and represented the human race which had lost appetite for God and His Spirit over the ages. We lost every form of desire for God's glory, with the depths for which we were created. Through the accomplishment of all things, Jesus went through the checklist of all requirements and restored our thirst for the original status; back to God's image and after His likeness, that we might forever be permanently and absolutely restored. He broke the divide so that we can receive fresh thirst for purity and holiness; enjoying the beauty of God's majesty, glory, intimacy and eternal restoration all over again.

He became thirsty so that we can become thirsty.

He became our sacrifice that could be accepted. He did it for us, so that we can enjoy prayer as originally designed, not as Seth who desired victory, but for us in the New Testament so that we can pray from victory not for victory. He said, it is finished. There's now therefore no condemnation, no condemnation, no condemnation, to them that are in Christ Jesus (Romans 8:1-2).

One of the most grievous pains is to be in God's presence and feel condemned. Through the victory given to us by the Most High God and His kindness the umbilical link between us and God is restored and paid for with an ultimate price by the Messiah's blood that speaks awesome things in agreement to

266

our prayers. We therefore pray for victory to activate what has already been provided and done for us. Our prayers today are full of thanksgiving, praise and appreciation, in the prevailing dynamics of laying hold of the finished work of the cross. New Testament prayer activates what is finished as well as provokes the inheritance of what has been provided. In the New Covenant, we are restored (as if it were) back to the Garden before the fall, with a much more intimate access to the Father than Adam enjoyed. The Bible says, where sin abounds, that is to say our human sins combined, God's grace much more abounds. Inferring that God restored us far beyond our original state. He also gave us more than what we lost. We have gained in limitless dimensions, with the promise to do exceedingly, abundantly, above all we can ask or think according to the power and grace that is deposited within us and for us, by the Holy Spirit.

The blockade of the devil is dealt with. The keys of hell and death and all its fear, removed. The contention between God and man, settled once and for all. Peace has come on earth and God's goodwill towards men is made manifest with evidences beyond proven records by Christ Jesus, our Brother, Friend, Messiah, Redeemer and the Bishop of Our Souls.

Every person called on this journey of one should lay hold on the necessity of praying from victory on a daily bases. It is the gateway that translates pain for provisions and that is needed for our success into physical reality. Your prevailing prayer life turns into manifestation what is yours in God's treasure house. Ask beyond limits, it shall be given beyond limits. Seek until it is released. Knock because you know that the door is Christ who has already prepared for you what you needed before you asked. You are the power of one in the hand of a faithful God who gives answers to your prayer as inheritance. Be blessed in your prayer life. Touch the heavens, change the world with this incredible technology of praying from victory to victory all the days of your life. You are the victorious one. In this journey it has already been decided, *it is finished*. As Christ finished it on the cross so we begin our journey with a finishing mindset, not looking back but looking ahead and making history. Make it BIG because of the provisions of the finished work of the cross. Receive the keys of prayer through Christ Jesus who loves you dearly. Therefore pray through what is provided for your purposeful accomplishment in your lifetime. Finish strong by praying through. Don't quit praying until the miracle is in your hand. Prayer includes thanksgiving, appreciation and declarations with faith that what you know is yours has already been given to you through your heritage, through in Christ.

The technology of prayer "in the name of Jesus" lifts you up above human levels. It makes you mount up with wings as the eagle and gives you prevailing instincts through the Holy Spirit to handle matters from the heavenly perspective. Your persistence in prayer gives you the platform for prevailing prayers at all times. Important as it is to have a financial breakthrough in business so it is essential to break through in prayer in the business of God's purpose. It draws you into God's power. Prayer pulls the throne of God into your world and the scenarios of concern. It changes the atmosphere of your vision.

Whatever is connected to prayer enjoys the limitless fire power of God's maneuvering grace for unprecedented breakthroughs. Don't just pray *about* things, rather pray *through* things. May you enjoy the fire power of engaging God in prayer through the ministry of the Holy Spirit that helps you navigate your course in God's world of productive purpose. Much prayer stirs much power and little prayer provokes little power. Your journey of destiny and leadership requires the clout of prayer which connects you to your cloud of exclusive vision.

THE PRAYER MANDATE OF LEADERSHIP

The most formidable leader this earth has ever known was and is Jesus. His influence transcends time and eternity, coming straight from heaven to lead the world into salvation, restoration, and glory. He is the most effective case study of a singular person whose journey of destiny, purpose and leadership outclasses all leaders from the beginning of time, through today, into the unimaginable future. Having the revelation of all things, as fully God and fully man, it is absolutely a wise thing to study His leadership style and key principles, which Christ held as a standard. One such principle and key He held dear to His heart was prayer. This incredible leader, in whom the Father was so well pleased, had a personal prayer life. There must be something about prayer that He knew about from heaven that made Him invest so much into it. In Luke 11:1 after one of His prayer sessions, His twelve disciples asked Jesus to teach them to pray as John the Baptist taught his disciples. This insight is necessary for our discussion today. Consider this, that the frame of the question had this content:

- Teach us to pray
- As John the Baptist taught his disciples

This request means prayer can be taught and *must* be taught by leadership to leaders. It implies therefore that there is an expectation for leadership to understand the world of prayer so as to teach it. I pray every individual leader, called of God, follows the footsteps of Christ, the author and finisher of our faith. If He did not brush aside prayer by creating other justifications, then we shouldn't give excuses either.

Prayer is not talking or chatting, but a deep cherished fellowship with God.

Prayer is of great value to heaven; giving it the ability to influence the earth. Our prayer puts material into the hands of God to work within the systems of the earth. Prayer activates partnership between the Creator and His worshipers. The subject of discussion demands focus, attention and respect to God, in whose presence we abide. The scripture states that it is the delight of God the Father, the Son and the Holy Ghost, to find absolute prayer in the house of the Lord in every nation on the planet. Prayer speaks and understands every language. No matter where your calling, industry, profession or destiny take you, prayer is designed to be effective. It is a virtual expectation of the Lord that whosoever is under His influence, should pray consistently.

270

In Luke 18:1 Jesus says again, "That men always ought to pray and not to faint." With His personally strong prayer life and the incredible tutorial He gave His disciples, it is understandable why He can truly say that men always out to pray with conviction. The earth is filled with so much ungodly spiritual interference in the human community that prayer is an imperative subject.

> *...Nevertheless when the Son of man cometh, shall he find faith on the earth?*   **Luke 18:8**

This means that Heaven considers persistence in prayer as a pointer to one's faith in God. If faith without works is dead, then one of the works of faith is a formidable praying culture developed by every God lover whose dream is to succeed extraordinarily in His calling and mandate. We continue to see the various aspects of the life of Jesus in prayer. The time of His baptism He was in prayer. On Mount Olivet while He prayed, He was transfigured into the most glorious personality ever seen by His disciples where His face shone as the light and His garments as the sun. In both praying scenarios, His Father's glory was revealed as He said, *In Thee I am well pleased.*

James the half-brother of Jesus, records in James 5:16, "The effectual fervent prayer of a righteous man avails much." This means that the active and passionate prayer of any righteous man produces great results. What are the chances that James' first and foremost reference point of a praying man was His own brother Jesus, whom he watched daily. Moved possibly by the unprecedented mega results of the prayer life of Jesus and His disciples who (He trained), James came to this veritable conclusion:

Focused prayers backed by the life of the Spirit of God, prevail extraordinarily.

If Christ did not joke with or about prayer, we should never second-guess its importance in the life of every one singular person whose journey into destiny must avail much. Statistics of very successful Christian leaders and mega ministers and ministries have revealed that if they were to have a second opportunity to start all over again, they would pray so much more than they had. King David, in Psalm 55:17 said, "Evening, morning and noon will I pray." May you advance on your journey with a reservoir of prayer and intercession following you. Prayer is the inspiration of leaders and all in whom God's love abides. It is therefore the product of love. Prayerlessness produces pride, hatred and enmity with God.

- John the Baptist had a prayer life, so also his disciples - LEADERS.
- Jesus Christ had a prayer life, so also His disciples who became apostles - LEADERS.
- The saints of God through Christ, who are God's kings and priests in the earth, ought to pray without ceasing - LEADERS.

May we fill the systems of the kingdom of God, with the prayer fire-power needed to prevail in these end-times. This is an incredible key in our hands, if we so desire to avail, prevail, inspire and have dominion. It is our mark of greatness to do what our Master Jesus did to change His world, our world, and generations to come, with an incredible standard and example of prayer. May you be that one singular person whose prayer fire-power transforms our world into the best community of leaders ever known.

CHAPTER 25:

THE BOOK OF GOD

God is an all time leader who never reads to learn but writes for all His prodigies to study. As an omnipotent, omnipresent, and omniscient Being, He is knowledge. It is important to state that He does not *have* knowledge but that He *is* knowledge. Having said this, anything you have can be taken away but who you are you do not lose; therefore your fellowship with Him, the all knowing God, makes you encounter knowledge. As His presence rubs off, you increase in the knowledge that He is. By inspiration in this love encounter with God, you grow in the grace of the revelation of who He is, ultimately giving you all it takes to walk with Him in understanding and therefore fulfilling your mandate for Him appropriately. Knowing Him makes you have Who He is.

God is all knowing, all powerful, and present everywhere at the same time. This fact being the truth He writes, reveals, inspires and pours out His Spirit in records of glory, to inform and educate creation. Being a leader He writes therefore setting the standard for all His leaders to be authors.

It is often said that leaders are readers, but I conclude that the next level of true leadership is authorship. Christ being the author and finisher of our faith, says it all. The uniqueness of generational leaders and patriarchs is that as they blaze the trail, they leave behind nuggets and footprints for *"success devotees"* to glean. It is therefore a thorough fact that leaders are authors. Luke the doctor, wrote the entire book of Luke and Acts to his leaders in training and Theophilus to set in order with perfect understanding things that happened of Jesus His life, death burial resurrection and legacy.

The entire Bible is the inspired Word of God which carries His will and reflects His nature and ways in accordance to history and creation. Proof is shown in the very records of God written in what I consider a book of His personal purpose as He deals with individual achievers and instruments of grace according to His personal relations; to *the power of one*.

A true and a formidable leader feeds the next generation with solid, inspirations that keep them on track with excellence and productivity. A leader lives what he writes and what he writes he leaves as a legacy for generations to come. This is to:

1) Establish a databank of truth, facts and values for the

next generation.

2) Put in order the chronicles of records, facts, events and experiences.

3) Make plain patriarchal visions and prophetic inspirations and directions.

4) Placard the syllabus of counsel, advice and admonishment to the present and future generations without end.

God is an author.

God is the author of creation and His Bible; this He did for all to read. However some records He has are not for our perusal but His alone. Such a book was spoken about by Moses in Exodus 32:32-34.

> *Yet now, if thou wilt forgive their sin and if not,*
> *blot me, I pray thee, out of thy book which thou hast*
> *written. And the Lord said unto Moses, Whosoever*
> *hath sinned against me, him will I blot out of my*
> *book.* **Exodus 32:32-33**

My question is, "How did Moses know that God had a confidential book written for Himself, concerning the affairs of the purpose as it relates to Moses' statement?" The backdrop of this event was in direct relations to Moses' purpose and mandate to take the Jews out of captivity into promise. A journey and a task that was literally impossible to man except by the full, dominant help of the architect of the project, the Lord. In the course of events, Aaron the high priest, who was placed in charge of the congregation as the assistant to Moses, caves into the pressure of the people and creates a man-made god in the likes of a golden calf. A device of man and not the purpose of God. In God's wrath to annihilate the people of Israel, God presents a proposal to Moses saying, "Let me destroy everyone and begin a new nation from you Moses alone. This was not an impossible inspiration to God because Moses knew that He had done this before. History was about to repeat itself when God wiped out the entire human race and began a new generation as in the days of Noah, in Genesis chapters six through nine. In that context God said, "My Spirit shall not continue to strive with man." Here again His Spirit was striving with man. The very ways of God showed Moses that something was up.

A true leader stands in the gap, creating pathways for direction with effective initiatives.

Turning on the intercessor in him, Moses engaged God with an appeal for mercy instead of judgment. He said to God, if You will destroy this people then all the kings in the wilderness will say You were not able to bring them into the land of promise effectively. It may not make us look good. But if you still desire to destroy them then kindly take my name from the book which you have written. Consider this: the first five books of the Bible were written by Moses the Pentateuch, meaning he was conversant with the inspirations that write the laws, and what we call today, the Bible events. I believe in spending intimate time with God on the Mountain top. Moses perceived the deeper things about God's ways. God has a personal book in which he collates what I believe to be His will, purpose, facts and outcomes of individuals He works with. Those who have achieved far beyond the average and on whose acts of obedience He could entrust purpose for strategic achievements and mandates which fit perfectly into His time tables; *The book you have written.*

The Lords response in Exodus 32:33-34:

Whosoever hath sinned against me, him will I blot out of my book.

- Therefore now go, *lead* the people unto the place of which I have spoken unto thee.
- Behold, mine angel shall go before thee.

My personal conviction behind this response is that the Bible is written for our admonishment, knowledge and revelation as a guide for all creation to abide by. It is also considered as the workbook and the Creator's manual of how to successfully live a life and manage creation. It is also for knowing who our God is and knowing who we are in Him. But the intimacy Moses had with God made him reveal to us that there is also what I may considered the "Achievers Book", which is a personal data chronicle in heaven not revealed to men.

In addition, Number 21:14 reveals that God has a book called "The Book of Wars," and Malachi refers to, "The Book of Remembrance." Both of these books are written by the Lord

Himself. This is very different than the generic inspiration that the Holy Spirit put upon apostles and prophets who wrote the Bible. In Psalm 40:7-8 King David says, "In the volume of the book it is written of me, *I delight to do thy will, O my God:* yea, thy law is within my heart.

The compilation of the thought process around God's books, seemed to be revealed around success stories of certain individuals. These books include:

- God's *Book of Wars*
- God's *Book of Remembrance*
- God's Book written of me (as stated by David) and
- *Your Book* (as spoken of by Moses)

The individuals include:

- Moses who crossed the Red Sea by the help of God, in a mega war scenario.
- David in his love for Israel, took on Goliath for the Lord's sake.
- Those who fear the Lord and think on His name continually (Malalchi 3:16).

Obeying God under exclusive demands suggests to me that God delightfully has a databank of His *Hall of Fame* recorded about the exploits of the righteousness in their time of life in the earth. Hebrews 11 reveals that, "By faith the elders obtained a good report before God and man." Faith has always been known to be the substance of things hoped for and the evidence of things not yet seen. Meaning that most of these people did not have the absolute provisions we do today, yet still had strong belief systems to do exploits.

- By faith, Abel offered unto God a more excellent sacrifice than Cain.
- By faith Enoch was translated that He should not see death.
- By faith Noah being warned of things to come, and moved with a godly fear, prepared an ark.
- By faith Abraham he was called to go out to the place to which he should receive his inheritance, obeyed.
- By faith Sarah received strength to conceive seed.
- By faith Isaac blessed Jacob and Esau concerning things to come.
- By faith Jacob when he was dying, blessed both sons of Joseph.
- By faith Joseph, when he died made mention of the departing of the children of Israel and commanded him to take along his bones with them.
- By faith the parents of Moses hid him for three months because they saw he was a proper child.
- By faith Moses refused to be called the son of Pharaoh's daughter, choosing rather to suffer affliction with the people of God then to enjoy the pleasures of sin for a moment.
- By faith they passed through the red sea as by dry land

and the Egyptians attempting to do so drowned.

- By faith the walls of Jericho fell down, as they circled about them seven days.
- By faith the harlot Rahab, perished not with them that believed not.
- By faith Gideon, Barak, Samson, Jeptha, David, Samuel, the prophets; who through faith subdued kingdoms, wrought righteousness, obtained promises, stopped the mouth of lions, quenched the violence of fire, escaped the edge of the sword, out of weakness were made strong, waxed valiant in fight, and turned to flight countless armies.
- By faith women received their dead raised to life again.
- By faith many survived cruel trials of mockings and scourgings, tortures and more.
- By faith many wandered about in sheep skin, goat skin; being destitute, afflicted and tormented, in deserts, in mountains, dens and caves of the earth, and yet all obtained good reports before the Lord.

In Moses' dialogue with God he said, "Lord if You will destroy these people then take my name from the book which You have written." I pray however you will not ask God to take your name out of the book He has written, because it's no fun. If God is a rewarded of those who diligently seek Him and take the high road to achievements then I can understand how He can have books written of facts, figures and results of His high achievers who refuse to subject themselves to the dainties and of excuses of life. It is the desire of God that we be conquerors and overcomers because that is who He is. Creating us in His image and after His likeness, we are expected as individuals, whom He chooses to walk and work with, to become the same. Let us Trust in all His divine abilities to make anything happen as He desires. Is there anything too hard for the Lord? For with God all things are possible to them that believe.

May your belief system be highly productive and firing on all its cylinders, defeating the gravitational pull of excuses, the status quo and religious passivity. Just as Moses refused to be called the son of Pharaoh's daughter and took on the *highway of purpose,* so can we! Apostle Paul, letting go the past and pressing in for the prize of the high calling, so can we! *The power of one* is a principle that attracts God's respect and joy. You can make it because you were designed to succeed. Having said all this, I believe it is possible for God to remove someone from His book who will sin against Him by disobedience. A case in point was a man in I Samuel 15:1-3 called King Saul.

> *Thus saith the Lord of hosts, I remember that which Amalek did to Israel, how he laid wait for him in the way, when he came up from Egypt. Now go and smite Amalek, and utterly destroy all that they have, and spare them not; but slay both man and woman, infant and suckling, ox and sheep, camel and ass.*
>
> **I Samuel 15:1-3**

I would like to explain further by saying that truly the gift and the callings of God are without repentance, which means when He calls you as an individual, you will forever be the called and chosen person for that job. It will never be revoked no matter your errors. But because of the timetables of God in which His purposes need to be fulfilled, it is possible for Him to keep your calling intact and yet still allow someone else to handle the assignment so that it would not fail. With this being said, as the Sovereign God who prefers mercy to judgment, with our repentance He is yet able to restore completely any person or even a generation. He is God.

But in this scenario God had a war of revenge against the Amekiltes, for which cause Moses had to keep his arms lifted from sunrise to sundown on Mount Rephidim. For over 300 years this war of God had to be fought physically of which Saul, the King of Israel was chosen. God decided this battle in eternal times, over three centuries before Saul was born. God appointed a time for that purpose, in His *Book of Wars*, and Saul was chosen to execute it.

By disobeying God, a series of events continued in Saul's life leading up to what eventually the scriptures declare as Saul having died as though he was never anointed. May such an equation be a perfect misfit in your life. May you never miss God by sinning against Him in total rebellion and stubbornness to desire our carnal dreams far above His perfect will and purpose.

In 2 Corinthians 10:4, Paul the Apostle states that the weapons of our warfare are mighty through God in the pulling down of strongholds. In the course of the power of one, there are battles we face, some based on the terrain of our calling, the inherited uncompleted assignments of the previous leaders of our time, or battles unknown to us but yet absolutely the design of God to address certain rebellions in the spirit, over destinies, time zones, and generations, etc. Exodus 15:3 declares that the Lord is a man of war, the Lord is His name. He therefore has a book of wars. Like Paul said, I fought the beast of Ephesus, but the Lord has been my stay. King David says, by my God I have run through a troop and by my God I have leapt over walls.

In Paul's letter to the church in Colossae and Laodicea in Colossians 4:17, he singles out a young apostle called Archippus instructing him to take heed to the ministry which he received in the Lord, that he may fulfill it. " It is God's greatest expectation and hope that you fulfill His purpose and not the devices of men. Kindly keep this in remembrance that both heaven and the earth as well as all creation have had an earnest expectation for your manifestation and therefore are watching with great cheers of hope. You can do this as that one chosen person. The hinges of the doors of eternity are connected to your obedience. You are highly anointed to excel. Believe it.

The Author and the Finisher of our faith is another title of Jesus our Savior and the pre-eminent one. He is also the complete set of God's purpose. I John 5:7 announces to all creation, the brain behind heaven's records.

For there are three that bear record in heaven, the Father, the Word, and the Holy Ghost: and these three are one.   **I John 5:7**

Designing this fact, the Triune God sets records in place, according to what is in Their minds and hearts in agreement as One. The language in which Their records are written is the language of the Word. By His Spirit, we are privileged to become instruments of God's writing. We become the living epistles of the book God has written, personally to Himself and in some cases, for those around us. It is a great blessing to know that we live the physical life which was authored by the Spirit of God thats dwells mightily within us.

May you be filled with the Holy Ghost to overflowing so as to reflect the very heartbeat of God and bring joy into this world, salvation to souls and direction that is badly needed today through salvation. It is written of you that you shall do the will of God. There is nothing that is more gratifying than this, but above all, as you fellowship with the Holy Spirit daily, you illuminate the Word with acts of Christ that speak through your words and lifestyle. Jesus said in Acts 1:8, "Thou shall be filled with power after that the Holy Ghost shall come upon you and you shall be my witnesses in to the uttermost parts of the earth."

Enjoy the inspiration of the Holy Spirit as your life reveals what has been authored. As Moses said in the book that you have written, so may we also say, "Lord keep me in that book and help me be a world changer according to the glorious baptism of Your person into my life." You are truly a new creation, according to what has been written. You can do all things through Christ according to what is written. May you choose to obey what is written of you in the *Book of God.*

CHAPTER 26:

GENTLENESS

History has proved that extraordinary first rated leaders, who have sought God as their source with all their hearts, have always found strength through the gentleness of Him whom they have come to know. By experience they have caught key revelations from His stature and majesty. In Psalm 18:35, King David confidently stated:

- Thou hast also given me the shield of thy salvation
- Thy right hand hath held me up
- Thy gentleness hath made me great

God's gentleness, derived from His nobility and majesty, rubs off on those who have always desired His presence. In the intrigue of knowing Him more, they end up catching key understanding as their lives get assimilated to the divine nature. In other words, there are grandeur attributes of God that are not necessarily taught, but caught when a man's heart is right with God. Out of the heart of God comes the issues of His divine life and as many as connect to the heart of fellowship with the Most High, naturally get pulled into the revelation of His nature, which incubates greatness in all who desire His ways above His acts.

The culture of greatness experienced by devout God-lovers has proven the authenticity of His gentleness by being able to inspire excellence, strength, and extraordinary transformation in people's lives. One of the greatness leaders of the Holy Scriptures, Moses, said in his dialogue with God:

> *Now therefore, I pray thee, if I have found grace in thy sight, shew me now thy way, that I may know thee, that I may find grace in thy sight and consider that this nation is thy people. And he said, My presence shall go with thee, and I will give thee rest. And he said unto him, if thy presence go not with me, carry us not up hence. For wherein shall it be known here that I and thy people have found grace in thy sight? Is it not in that thou goest with us? So shall we be separated, I and thy people, from all the people that are upon the face of the earth.*

> **Exodus 33:13-16**

His reference is the fact that the greatness found in him as a leader and the distinguished personality of the Hebrew family sojourning through the wilderness was a result of the overwhelming impact of God's prevailing presence. The presence of God, which comprises of all that He is, has, and does has an incredible power to transform ordinary people into greatness in stature, ability, and performance. In King David's experience, he stated, "Thy gentleness has made me great (Psalm 18:35)."

It is the most understandable style of thinking that the anointing from God creates supernatural ability in the life of every one person endowed by the grace of strength. David with such a crave to seek God on a consistent basis, comes out with a revelation very unusual from the normal insightfulness of God. He expresses His greatness as the result of God's gentleness; an amazing thought process for every leader or aspiring champion of the cause of righteousness to meditate upon. Greatness, born out of gentleness, puts a twist to the impactful thought of God, making somebodies out of nobodies. The gentleness of God makes great those who serve Him in spirit and truth.

Years ago, during a leadership conference in the Northwestern part of America, the line up of speakers included Dr. Yonggi Cho of Yoido, South Korea. So much had been said about him and especially on his book, The Fourth Dimension, stirred up my intrigue to hear him speak. After an incredible time of worship and the singing of glorious songs to the Lord, the master of ceremonies of the conference introduced the guest speaker, Dr. Cho. A very petite personality, yet with an outstanding and grandiose testimony, of pastoring the largest church in the world at that time with almost one million people in his congregation, my expectation was even much more heightened for an exuberant preaching. When he took the microphone, the gentleness with which he accepted the respectful introduction of his person and his honorable expression of love, to the hosts of the conference and the audience, set the stage for his message. In his opening statement he said, "I would like to acknowledge my Best Friend and Senior Partner, The Holy Spirit, for whose reason and ministry, we are all gathered here today.

The power of God that covered the entire conference through this incredible gentleness of speech and demeanor, caused me to weep through out the message without control. Tears raced through my eyeballs without my permission, as my spirit and soul were arrested by the blanket cloud of God's thick presence that sat upon this large crowd, as greatness was released through gentleness. The tears flowed out of my eyes, strength was increased and for as long as this message was going on, the glory of God was so strong upon me, as tho I was put back on creation table for a renovation of my being in God's presence. The impartation of God's virtues in my life, were the results of the tears that were coming out of my life. As if something had to go out, for something more precious to come in. Having said that, tears are also a sign of hitting the maximum of your capacity. In this dimension it was more of strength for strength, converging on a weak soul, who had the hunger for God's presence. I believe that God gave me, a heart for leadership that I never had and a capacity that has helped me through my journeys on this earth up to date. His presence is heaven to us. I recommend that every true leader on this planet would learn to abide in His divine atmosphere and to cocoon themselves in God's presence. It is from that gentle place that we are able to mount up with wings as an eagle, for vision, mastery, excellence and glory. Truly its not by power, not by might, but by the Holy Spirit. It is important to also note that one of the fruit, of the Holy Spirit is gentleness (Gal. 5:22-23).

This mystery is the greatest attribute to be found in every God-centered leadership and network. The highest level of activity and performance is gentleness as a result of God's confident greatness that is allowed to have dominion. When the weight of God's presence sits upon a people, His gentleness which is devoid of fear and anxiety becomes pre-eminent. Gentleness produces greatness and greatness feeds on gentleness to produce unshakable results and unquestionable breakthroughs. It is a matured state of faith life revealed through seasoned and tested leadership and leaders. Gentleness comes as an understanding as well as a virtue when the mighty hand of God rests upon a person or a people, in a given point in time. Truly it is an attribute of the divine nature of which we are partakes (2 Peter 1:4). The dealings of God through the trials of our faith overtime can also produce gentleness. After all is said and done and after you have seen it all and gone through it all, your spirit becomes tempered with the truth that God lives and He lives indeed in you. The interplay of meekness and gentleness in leadership is a priceless fruit to bear. It makes you unshakable, indestructible, immovable and yet potent with the fervent power for excellent performances and results. Gentleness is deep and makes you drink of the deep wells of God's glory and nature as in Psalm 42:7, "deep calls unto deep…"

This is to say a gentle spirit is never disturbed by outside influences so it can focus on weightier matters to produce weightier results of life, for the greatest impact on a generation through one person. Gentleness makes me great.

For the kind of things life puts you through, in your pursuit to obey God, the end result can only be a solid and well grounded leader, with no room for doubt and unbelief. Your patience is at this point, stretched and renewed by that spine of steal that lifts you above the storm. Gentleness produces steadiness of life which puts you in the first three brackets of the most outstanding leaders and leadership, in the category of the type-A personality group of trail blazers. The gentleness of God as revealed in His sovereign personality as the Most High, rubs off on those seek to always abide in His presence. The presence of God is the atmosphere that produces such attributes as gentleness and strength. It's not about age of a person, but the spirit of a person, that is broken out of weakness into strength. It rubs off on your spirit, as you fellowship with God who is a Spirit. His gentleness makes you smart, wise, gracious and trustworthy.

In Numbers 12:3-8 we see the remarkable testimony of the man Moses who had a deep walk with God for a forty year period. The testimony of Him says, he became the meekest man in the earth.

*Now the man Moses was very meek, above all the
men which were upon the face of the earth.*

Numbers 12:3

Meekness is interwoven with the nature of gentleness but
devoid of weakness. A meek person is sober as well as a gentle
spirit, but usually full of the saturation of unbelievable fervency
and strength. It makes you despise the storm by a set mind of
believing God. It is that inert awareness that God is in charge
and there is nothing to worry about. Whatever He says He will
do He will do. It is also a clear sign that you have a consistent
deep walk in the depths of the Holy Spirit of God. The results
dimension of such a state can be nothing less than off the charts
and far above the aggregate of every human average.

Gentleness, out of the word gentle, is defined as: considerate
and kindly, not steep or sudden, gradual, well born, noble, and
to raise to the status of a noble. In Psalm 18:35, David states that
God's gentleness has made him great. It is noteworthy to see that
this was not God saying that His gentleness will make David
great, rather it is David's experience that opened the file of a discovery that there is something about God's gentleness that produces greatness. It is the kind of thing that draws the picture as
though David discovered this insight in his laboratory of search-
ing after God. There are things we discover as we glean endlessly with rapt attention with one singular goal of the passion to
know God. What King David meant is that the considerations,
and concessions of God granted him the space of development

needed for the stature of greatness heaven required before the foundation of the world. The incredible kindness of God, in the coaching method of His beloved who are determined to stick to the pattern of the call imprinted on their spirit, is outstanding. Such considerations are usually based on God's ultimate expectation desired for a person, knowing very well what He wants to produce. The architect of time finishes His plan and purpose in the volumes of the book He writes for each individual.

> *Then said I, Lo, I come: in the volume of the book it*
> *is written of me, I delight to do thy will, O my God:*
> *yea, thy law is within my heart.*   (Psalm 40:7-8)

The awareness of your purpose as graphically imprinted in God's eternal plan for you creates a restfulness yet a passionate determination to fulfill that which is expected by eternity. Such revelation of your mandate creates gentleness. In other words, the gentleness of God your Creator is transferred int your spirit as a fruit producing tendency for perfection.

He knows what He intends to do with that person and therefore backs their journey with a great heart of consideration of several options designed to secure His chosen ones for an ultimate success story, to His glory. It is said those who He did predestinate, He calls; those that He calls, He justifies; those that He justifies, He glorifies (Romans 8:30).

God's gentleness proceeds out of His confident assurance in himself, "That which I have begun to do in this person shall come to a fulfilled end." He is considerate; not based on our weaknesses or strengths, but rather on His omnipotent stately stature, bringing fulfillment and success without fail. He considers His own ability to make all things work together for our good for which cause truly gentleness can produce greatness. Greatness defined as:

- Larger than others of the same kind
- Remarkable or outstanding in magnitude, degree or extend
- Superior in quality or character
- Grand
- Very skillful
- First rate

The gentleness of a leader produces greatness in those being led.

This amazing revelation came out of the observation of an outstanding leader whose experience with God gives us an amazing principle of leadership. The day when God exposed His intention publicly about David, the humble shepherd boy, He commandeered the prophet Samuel to anoint him with oil from a horn. This great ceremony took place in the presence of elders of Bethlehem in his family's house. 1 Samuel 16:13 in the scriptures recalls when the anointing came upon David's head. It separated the young man from his past and future, being captured in the phrase *"from that day forward."* In other words, David's journey into greatness began when the oil of God was released upon him as a symbol of the Spirit of God. Noting fervently that one of the attributes of the fruit of God is gentleness; one can say the gentle Spirit of the gentle God produced such maturity and grace in the young man. It produced in him such a behavioral greatness and such a transformed stature that no one could ignore from that day forward. For that matter, it was not so much about what David would do, but much more what he would become. Truth be told, *who you are* is more important than *what you do* because your acts truly reflect your nature. From that day forward, David's great deeds reflected his greatness. My late father, David Ziga, of blessed memory, always said to his children that, "A man should not live in years but in deeds."

The journey of a reconstructed heart of a leader, whose life has been touched by God, always produces depths which inspire the search for more of God.

In Psalm 42, the son of Jesse who began to search for ALL of God, revealed in his writing that, deep calls unto deep. In every case where the Spirit of God has come upon people, it can be seem as the *greatness-creating-power* of the gentle and the *all wise God. It* often overwhelms ordinary people to begin extraordinary journeys of amazing dimensions.

Acts 2:12 says, "That they were all amazed and were in doubt saying to one another what meanest this?" Speaking the language of God is a clear attribute of the productivity of God's stately nature. Revealed in Acts 2:11, these ordinary folks heard the wonderful works of God in their own tongues and speech. It is impossible to separate the lingo and the words of a man from his inner nature. Wise men speak wise things; foolish men make silly utterances, but great men as produced by God, speak the wonderful works of the great nature of God.

David found favor and proclaimed that, "Thy gentleness has made me great!" I pray this statement echoes in the life of all those that journey through the pages of this book; understanding that there is a truly great God whose greatness and gentleness makes Him take human form (Jesus), without the sense of risking His glory. He does this to impart into us His eternal treasures of noble and stately characteristics. In other words, the voluntary descent of the Most High God in His graciousness to connect and affect the inferior fallen nature of man shows His deep love for us. Show me a gentle leader with an assured and considerate demeanor and I will show you the kind of first rated and skillful spiritual sons, daughters and leaders He molds after Himself.

- Gentleness produces greatness
- Great leaders produces gentle leaders
- There is greatness in gentleness

I therefore dare to challenge sound leaders to believe that true greatness must be covered in the spirit of gentleness and nobility. Gentleness is considered as the fifth of the nine stately fruits of the Spirit of God recorded in the book of Galatians.

But the fruit of the Spirit is love, joy, peace, longsuffering, gentleness, goodness, faith, Meekness, temperance: against such there is no law.

Galatians 5:22-23

Gentleness being the fifth, which is the number for grace, carries in itself an extraordinary ingredient of God's grace to empower anyone who loves God to become great achievers, movers, and shakers in His Kingdom. The nine dynamic fruitful manifestations of God's divine attributes become components of greatness in God; that is to say love, joy, peace, longsuffering, gentleness, goodness, faith, meekness, and temperance reveal the table of contents of the subject of greatness in God's language. Gentleness is found in those who fellowship with Him continually. A truly great mind in God must relevantly display this fruit.

Gentleness feeds into meekness. Matthew 5:5 declares that the meek shall inherit the earth. This certainly is a truth producing factor of people well-tempered by the glory of God, into the immovable stately stature of first rate standards, unbeatable by any law.

In Numbers 12:3, Moses, another example of a devotion after God, grows from a violent young man into a stately first-rated leader in God's presence, to the extent of being considered by Him as the meekest man on earth. Considering gentleness and meekness as fruit of the spirit clears the way for every true servant of God to become great by His gentleness and graciousness. Paul, another violent militant fanatic, formerly known as Saul, through his experience in God's presence, discovers a new and stately passion of celebrating the loss of all things in life, that he might know Christ and the power of His resurrection, to be made conformable into His image. The theme of this book, *The Power of One*, is to let those in this generation understand that God creates a playing field for all to attain possibility and success according to divine standards, if only we choose to be serious in Him. God raises one person and develops out of that one, a powerful witness of a manifest success story of the of the most extraordinary kind without partiality. For God is not a respecter of persons but a respecter of diligence. May your diligence grant you greatness before the omnipotent, gentle God whom all creation reveres.

> *It is the spirit that quickeneth; the flesh profiteth nothing. The words that I speak unto you, they are spirit, and they are life.* **John 6:63**

Jesus Christ said it is the Spirit that quickens and the flesh profits nothing. Of all flesh and blood that walked on this earth, there was none more gentle than Christ. Fully God and fully man made him the all-time best gentleman that ever lived. Gentleness as to nobility caused kings to shake in their boots standing in His presence. If you are truly born of God and filled with God's spirit, men must fear you for the stately stature of the divine that is magnificently revealed by His Holy Spirit through you. In Luke 2:52 it is said of Jesus at the age twelve that He grew in wisdom, stature, and favor with God and man. If the gentleness of Jehovah made David great, then the same goes for us. The gentleness of Jesus Christ and His Holy Spirit transforms us into true servants of God, walking in His limelight, making us great.

To be great is to be larger than others; skillful and superior in quality of character. These are the dimensions that are attainable through God as we represent Him through the earth as His sons and daughters walking in the heritage of Christ our Savior. In the spirit of humble servitude we are mighty in the pulling down of ungodly strongholds and establishing Godly strongholds.

The life of King David is a solid example of the power of one as it relates both to the Old and the New Testament. His kingship was outstanding and exemplified the metaphor of the Messiah and His throne. Referred to as the Son of David, Jesus also called Himself the Root of David and the Bright and Morning Star. The devotion of King David and his passion to seek after the Lord His God is very intriguing. He walked in revelation as a king, a prophet, a worshiper, a general of war, a parent, a husband and a patriarch. There is no other king in the bible that was anointed three times, having five covenants like this incredible son of Jesse.

Imagine David, a naturally born eighth son of his physical family and yet adopted by God Almighty as a firstborn to the extent that in the genealogy of Christ, David is considered as a patriarch before Abraham in the book of Matthew.

The book of the generation of Jesus Christ, the son of David, the son of Abraham.   **Matthew 1:1**

Higher than the kings of the Earth, and in the first class of leadership called by God into a first-born state of being, David finds favor through the gentleness of God. This is an outstanding act of unspeakable favor and elevation. God speaks about David in Psalm 89:27 saying, "I will also make him my firstborn higher than the kings of the earth."

In the event that God makes a shift in a man's life like this, it's a true revelation of the Most High putting emphasis on His intentional favor and high calling on a man. Such weight of glory and mandate register incredible placement in the heart of God for duty, calling, and purpose. The truth is that every born again believer has received the same kind of position of firstborn-ship in God through Christ Jesus just as David. We are today, through the Holy Spirit, enjoying the very placement that only the firstborns in God get to walk in. If Christ is the firstborn of all creation and the first begotten of God, then all who walk in Christ become joint-heirs of the firstborn privilege. Therefore, we can also say the gentleness of Jesus has made us great. As we walk in His Spirit, we produce spiritual sons and daughters of greatness due to the Spirit of gentleness that works mightily within us.

God states in Psalm 89:29 that David's throne shall be as the days of heaven and in verses 36-37, as the sun before Him and the faithful witness in heaven. The greatness of this king on the throne virtually responded to his revelation and fellowship with God which is actually how it ought to be. A person can never be greater than his revelation of the master he serves. It is an incredible activity of God's grace that enables you to understand His authority and purpose. David, being the very celebrated icon of the Jewish state, also produced one of the wisest and richest kings in human history known as Solomon; the other name given to him by Nathan the prophet, was Jedidiah. With all this in perspective, King David, in addition to God's gentleness making him great, enunciates in Psalm 18:28-34:

- For thou wilt light my candle: the LORD my God will enlighten my darkness.
- For by thee I have run through a troop; and by my God have I leaped over a wall.
- As for God, His way is perfect: the word of the LORD is tried: He is a buckler to all those that trust in him.
- For who is God save the LORD? Or who is a rock save our God?
- It is God that girdeth me with strength, and maketh my way perfect.
- He maketh my feet like hinds' feet, and setteth me upon my high places.
- He teacheth my hands to war, so that a bow of steel is broken by mine arms.

It is important to record that to Jesse, a son was born called David, but to God greatness was instituted.

In all our attaining, may we desire gentleness in God, not passivity but the stature born of His spirit; a tremendous reflection of a new creation through Christ. David said, "The gentleness of God produced greatness in me." I do believe that the power of one man into greatness sets the individual on the pathway of greatness, not by what he achieves but by the impartation from the Most High God into his life. The best transformation of a person is that which begins from within revealed to the outside.

Anointed at a private event, as one man before the audience of his father, his seven brothers, and the elders of Bethlehem, was only the beginning. Publicly, David had to face Goliath as one man before the audience of two powerful armies: Israel and Philistine.

There is always a private side of a public leader in God. The decree to which your private depths run, is the degree to which your public success shall echo. Referring to God's gentleness that made him great, David is saying the nobility of God and His considerate kindness towards him made him first rated. This revelation of humility should be made into a case study for all leaders. If the gentleness of God, whom David served as a servant, birthed greatness out of the son of Jesse, then it behooves the gentleness of David to produce greatness also among those whom he ruled over.

The principle of greatness born out of gentleness, is an all-time, high-profile, success story producer.

Wise servants don't take advantage of gentle and great leaders. They rather receive impartation, strength, and virtue from the same. The power of one man called of God shall attain the highway of greatness through gentleness. Maturity in God makes you sober, meek, and gentle; *the power of one man in the hands of a gentle God.*

———m———

CHAPTER 27:

THE EXTENSION OF TIME

Time is an essential commodity in the sight of God and all who align themselves to His purpose. Created on the fourth day, in Genesis 1:14, God connected the first three days and the last three days of creation with time in the middle, influencing all the activities of the seven days from that day forward. It is the cardinal yet invisible spine that holds purpose together on this earth. It is also the vein through which purpose flows into the earth from eternity.

In Genesis 8:22 the Creator of heaven and earth said that while the earth remains, seed-time and harvest, cold and heat, summer and winter, day and night shall not cease. The exposition of this fact was a mystery revealed as to how God ordained seed, harvest, cold, heat, summer, winter, day, night and seasons to function effectively. Therefore saying there is a seed time, there is a harvest time, there is a cold time, there is a summer time, there is a day time and there is a night time. So long as time exists, the elements of purpose shall be fulfilled. Having said that, God also meant that the extension of time brings closure to the seasonal bunch of purpose and expectation. It does not matter how big the harvest is, its fulfillment is dependent on apportioned time.

The outpouring of great grace upon everybody who is called requires time for manifestation. In other words, since grace is an empowerment to produce results above human ability, time to do the work is of prime essence. The productivity of grace is so huge that the cutting off of time or its wasting can be an eternal tragedy to your relevance. It's like flying an airplane made by the Boeing manufacturing company, but not having an adequate run-way to land it safely. There are several cases in life where, due to our ignorance of God's will, time has been wasted on frivolous things. The prodigal son squandered his resources in a prime time of his life. In the re-awakening of his positive consciousness, one of the greatest pains possibly in His heart could be how much time he misused, missing out on valuable opportunities that could have produced results, that befit his status.

On his return to His father's house he said, "Father I have sinned against God and against you." Sinning against God was a conviction of mishandling the reason he was created, but against his father, was the conviction of dishonoring the heritage. If there would be any one desire in his mind, it might be to request the extension of time to undo what he had done.

In John 11:35 Jesus wept at the funeral of Lazarus. Certainly He was a dear friend to that family because the Bible says so, but could it also be that an unfortunate mischief stole away Lazarus' time on earth, hence depriving him from fulfilling the major purpose of God. Jesus wept. Possibly, His heart broke in the tragedy of a strong man, a good person, having all it takes to finish his course, suddenly lost his time. I would have wept too knowing very well that purpose was tied up with time. Therefore the resurrection of Lazarus extended His time on the earth to finish his assignment.

In John 12:9-11 the Bible actually says that many came to that same city, not to see Jesus but to see Lazarus who was resurrected. People said, lets go see a man whose time was extended on earth to finish his cause. So much attraction came to Lazarus to glorify God, more than the presence of Jesus, who did the miracle. Taking this even further, the impact of the works of Jesus so much defused the inept skeptical stand of the Pharisees and religious powers. This outstanding role of leadership by Jesus caused even his avowed enemies to conclude that the world cannot be stopped from following Jesus. Truly no weapon formed against Him prospered. John 12:19 says, "The Pharisees therefore said among themselves, perceive ye how you prevail nothing, behold the world has gone after him."

The extension of time on earth for Lazarus took the global awareness and acceptance of the ministry of the Messiah to another level. God showed Lazarus mercy and helped him in the extension of time, therefore he was privileged to finish what he was born for, which was to bring glory to God in an exceptional way. Through this the religious skeptics of the day were forced to accept their folly in acknowledging the authenticity of Jesus. The job can ultimately get done with the extension of time. Now that you know what you were born for, may God extend your time. If sickness and disease seem to be threatening your purpose, may God overrule the ungodly judgments over your soul. May the supreme court of God reverse the limitations placed upon you through faults of yours or others. May your ignorance, innocence and guilt be pardoned with the extension of time to finish your God given calling.

> *He asked life of thee, and thou gavest it him, even*
> *length of days for ever and ever.*   **Psalm 21:4**

As we all appeal for the extension of days, may God lengthen our valuable time, with the major outpouring of heaven's help in every area of your life. This mystery of grace is an advantage giver to prime time leaders whose hearts are sold out to love God, love His people and fulfill His counsel with a passion.

In Luke 19:41-44 as Jesus arrived in Jerusalem, He wept over the city which had refused the help of God and therefore missed their time of visitation and relevant moment of purpose. It is an unfortunate subject matter to have so much to offer and yet no time. Only God knows how many wealthy ideas and how much glory lies buried in the grave yard, because of the expiration of time. May God deliver us from this regret and advance us with the joy of mercy.

King Hezekiah cannot be ignored in this equation who was given the prophetic word to get his house in order in Isaiah 38:1-8. In his appeal to God for mercy, God extended his days for fifteen more years and confirmed it by resetting the sun dial ten degrees backwards. Oh what favor time can bring. What a blessing time can present in the life of people consumed with passion to do exploits with the God they have come to know. In my minds eye, I see the gavel of God in heaven hitting the judgment table, declaring upon you the extension of time. Run this race, avoid the pitfalls and finish your course. May your time on this earth be covered by the glory of God as a fetus is hidden in the womb of a mother. Time is precious.

It is imperative to comprehend the fact that the downloading of time into our hands can be a seal and a guarantee for achievement. This may also include the truth that there is "your time" and "me time" which is to say, for instance:

Abraham Lincoln's time

John F. Kennedy's time

Margaret Thatcher's time

Indira Gandhi's time

Ben Gurion's time

Golda Meir's time

Kwame Nkrumah's time

Nelson Mandela's time

George W. Bush's time

Apostle Paul's time

Billy Graham's time

Paul Crouch's time

I pray that if for any reason you feel convicted for not spending your time well or wisely, may the cry for the extension of time be your portion and may God answer this clarion call now.

> But thou, O Lord, shall endure forever; and thy remembrance unto all generations. Thou shalt arise, and have mercy upon Zion: for the time to favor her, yea, the set time, is come. **Psalm 102:12-13**

There is a mandate in God's command to add value to your time by increasing favor per second to your life so as to help your restoration and manifestation aright. Intelligent men and women with knowledge for witty inventions, cease to make a difference, if time is not given to them. *Lord bless and extend my time!*

For every person and every specific purpose which God designed, He made a time component, as a complete package to reveal His deep counsel and His limitless glory. Everybody and everything's purpose is to fit within the frame of time given for fulfillment, just as a glove fits one's hand. The incredible act and ways of God as revealed in the entire creation and its management has by all standards proven that there is no God like Jehovah, who deemed it fit and graciously gave everybody He brings to the earth, an opportunity to excel and fulfill a role.

As the scripture has said, righteousness and justice are the foundations of His throne (Psalm 89:14). He endows us all with talents, gifts, mandates and privileges to make all things beautiful according to what He planned for our lives. To imagine the capacity given to us individually by His partnership with us! All we can really say is, "Lord, extend our time and our days!" Not only because of the possibility of wasting time in the past, but His ability to show us mercy by restoring and renewing our time. May God extend your time by adding more years to you and increasing your anointing to do limitlessly more in one moment of time, so as to catch up with lost opportunities. May your prayer become:

"Lord, redeem my time and extend my days to achieve Your counsel without fail!"

In Ecclesiastes 3:1 the scripture says that under the heavens there is a season for everything and a time for every purpose. Time as to duration, is attached to every agenda from God on this earth. The greatness of the agenda determines the amount of time required. The relevance or irrelevance of a vision or a dream, determines how much value is appointed and therefore (after grasping your purpose and receiving the blessings of God) the time to fulfill it. He who prays for time prays for life. The very purpose of your life on this earth requires partnership with time. For every purpose there is a time, which means for every time available there must be a reason or a purpose. It is therefore imperative to be purpose-driven and time-sensitive.

Ecclesiastes 3:11 states that in God's time He makes all things beautiful. This shows how effectively God employs time to accomplish His glorious deeds. Beauty in God therefore is in the hands of time. I pray for God to bless and increase your time. With all that He has for you to do and the multitude of thoughts in His mind for you, time is what you need.

SECURITY

King David said, in Psalms 21:4, "He asked life of thee, and thou gavest it him, even length of days for ever and ever." The extension of life is therefore considered as one of God's greatest blessings upon a man, a people, or a generation. The relevance of the hidden gifts in you become beneficial to God and man with the extension of your time. When a man dies it is believed and hoped that he must have finished all his purpose according to the will of God. If he is killed, he is considered to be "cut off" before his time apportioned. This subject makes security, protection and covering very important. We need to be protected so as to finish our work in our time of life.

I had finished a conference, years ago in Ohio at a Christian Businessmen's Breakfast event and an elderly gentleman in his late 70's drew close to me with tears in his eyes. He held my necktie, pulled my face to his face and said, "Young man, I wish I knew the Lord at your age, but I delayed my journey to serving the Lord until a very old age. I now have so much passion to walk with the Lord but no strength because of the weakness age has given to me."

Although I prayed for this gentleman, he registered an indelible signal in my mind, which is the possibility of wasting one's precious time. Wasted years, I believe, can be the most abundant factor in everybody's life. It is highly probable that if there were a warehouse to pile up wasted years and another one to pile up useful years, to our surprise we may have many more warehouses to build, into which we would attempt to compress the countless time wasted. I have come to note that in every generation, the prosperity of the masses has always depended on the effectiveness of the few, whose time well spent has produced valuable contribution to feed the masses with help, direction and support. In the midst of this all, we see the goodness of God revealed in the book of Joel.

> *And I will restore to you the years that the locust hath eaten, the cankerworm, and the caterpillar, and the palmerworm, my great army which I sent among you.*   **Joel 2:25**

Would it be a surprise to imagine that the God who made time can heal it, restore it and extend it?

If you are called of God but have delayed your response, no matter what industry of relevance, I hope you will jump off the fence-sitting lifestyle into the center stage of purpose and duty. This elderly gentleman suggested to me that 90% of his life on this earth was lived in the world of wasted time, wasted dreams, wasted purpose and no fulfillment. He also never tasted the beauty and the joy of obeying the instructions of his Maker.

Value your time and utilize it purposefully to the glory of God, especially in the framework of His sovereign counsel for which you are created. A German philosopher once said, "What use am I, if I am not of use to God?" Ladies and gentlemen and fellow students of time, if time is what we need as a tool to fulfill the purpose of God, our hearts cry should be, *Lord give me life and extend my days!*

The parable of Luke 13:6-9 is an incredible pointer to this truth, the vine-dresser said in verse 8, "let it alone this year also, till I shall dig about it and dung it…" The owner of the vineyard was determined to cut it off, because of its fruitlessness and wastage of life, but the intercession of the vineyard keeper, indirectly, bought extra time for this tree to bear fruit. We are trees of righteousness in God's Kingdom vineyard. To the extent by which we have wasted the anointing and fruit-bearing, due to carelessness, etc. I pray that heaven gives us the extension of time and to cause a fresh anointing of the Holy Spirit to rejuvenate and replenish us to bear fruit. It is the law of the second chance. May you receive this grace now, beyond limits.

In Psalm 90 Moses says:

> *Lord, thou hast been our dwelling place in all generations. Before the mountains were brought forth, or ever thou hadst formed the earth and the world, even from everlasting to everlasting, thou art God.* **Psalm 90:1-2**

The days of our years are threescore years and ten; and if by reason of strength they be fourscore years, yet is their strength labor and sorrow; for it is soon cut off, and we fly away. Who knoweth the power of thine anger? even according to thy fear, so is thy wrath. So teach us to number our days, that we may apply our hearts unto wisdom. O satisfy us early with thy mercy; that we may rejoice and be glad all our days. Make us glad according to the days wherein thou hast afflicted us, and the years wherein we have seen evil. Let thy work appear unto thy servants, and thy glory unto their children. And let the beauty of the Lord our God be upon us and establish thou the work of our hands upon us; yea, the work of our hands establish thou it.

Psalm 90:10-17

It is essential to capture the inspiration that drove Moses to make such impactful utterances in prayer before the people he led. In a simple summary, coming to know God in the way revealed to him made him see the incredible limitation of man to control his own time. In other words, the majestic responsibility of the Most High God gives us grace to work according to His plan and purpose. Failing to comprehend the weight of God's glory and His impact on us to establish and manifest His purpose within the short time given to us, will cause any person to mishandle his time in life.

In his cry for help Moses said, Lord teach us to number our days that we may apply our hearts unto wisdom. *The phrase, teach us to number our days,* reveals the pain of wasted years and time on vanity. The focus on irrelevant agendas is the propagation of time-wasting theories. It is important for every purpose driven personality to value time given.

David in his cry to God for protection from his enemies, wisely said, "Lord my times and my seasons are in your hand." In other words the threat of his enemies to steal his time by attacking him, wishing to kill him, caught his attention so severely that he felt very inadequate to be a custodian of his own time. He appeals to greater authority as the best preserver and dispenser of time given.

- May God extend your days and preserve your time as long as you need it to finish your cause.
- May the Lord preserve your cause and order your steps in the incredible duration of expectation, attached to your life.

Man is pressured by the world of eternal expectation and the physical tangible world of the living every time there is breath in our nostrils. Whereas heaven is expecting you to fulfill the agenda for which cause you were sent onto the earth, the world and society in which you find yourself, have their own demands on your life. It is your prerogative as to which of the two you'll lean on for service. Do you spend your time serving God's eternal plans His way? Or do spend your time serving the social expectations the carnal way?

The depth of understanding your purpose and time, schools your choices and desires. Your scale of preference gets quickly amended when you are illuminated to see beyond the logical equation of life. Sometimes we see time and life within the scope of today and in the now whereas we ought to be seeing it far beyond the mundane culture of living.

If Ecclesiastes 3:15 says, "That which hath been is now; and that which is to be hath already been" and God requires that which is past, then it is important for us to be careful how we handle time. This truth revealed by Solomon in his later days is to reveal the programing of time by eternity in the framework of deeds and demands. *That which has been is now* means that everything we see today has already existed or the manifestation of all activities today were determined long time ago in eternity. The phrase, *that which is to be hath already been* refers to future events already completed in the spirit before their time of revelation in the natural. Whoever is suppose to be the next president of America has already been determined by God. In addition, whatever job description you will discover, as it falls on your lap ten years from today, has already been determined. This statement does not imply chaos, but rather the highest sense of organization, effectiveness, monitor, control and excellence.

Truly Hebrews 11:3 reveals that the world we see today came out of the world we don't see. I dare introduce to you an amazing God who knows the end from the beginning and therefore determines and plans things according to His perfect counsel.

What a Leader to serve!

God speaks in the book of Isaiah:

> *Remember the former things of old: for I am God,*
> *and there is none else; I am God, and there is none*
> *like me, declaring the end from the beginning, and*
> *from ancient times the things that are not yet done,*
> *saying, My counsel shall stand, and I will do all my*
> *pleasure. Calling a ravenous bird from the east, the*
> *man that executeth my counsel from a far country:*
> *yea, I have spoken it, I will also bring it to pass; I*
> *have purposed it, I will also do it.* **Isaiah 46:9-10**

God declares the end from the beginning. He also declares from ancient times things that are not yet fulfilled. All this He does according to the deep, wise counsel of His pleasure. He calls men therefore from any part of the earth to execute what He determined and proclaimed in ancient times that His purpose shall stand. These great statements of the Lord reveal the depths of His thoughts and the excellent perfection with which He executes His purpose, plans and strategies without fail. He is also revealing to us that when He calls a man to do a job for Him, He first finishes the job. Conclusively deciding what it is, how it must be executed and what results He wants out of it before making the "called" aware of His intentions. This is to say, The power of one man in the hand of God is effectively decided in all its parameters of operations and demarcated for Himself. This intriguing and trusting approach by God for every called person, beckons our obedience to the 'T'. Having said that, these scriptural propositions are announcing to every one man which God lays hands on that:

- He knows exactly what He wants out of you.
- He knows exactly what you need to do.
- He knows exactly how to handle every situation.
- The expectations of the end of your story and your days are already decided.
- God means business when He calls one man into partnership.

The wisest thing to do is to lean *not* on your understanding but in all your ways acknowledging Him. It is important to wait upon Him for inspiration and direction. Your future with God is already decided but the scope of fulfillment is within the power of our choice and includes choosing to let what God wants in you to come to pass through you. I must add, there is also a day of reckoning when an account will be given as to whether what heaven sent you to do, was done or not.

Ecclesiastes 3:15 also says that, "God requires that which is past." The scriptures imply that God requires out of every one person He calls, a fulfillment based on what was decided in ancient times for a reward. On the final day, it shall be said that you were born to fulfill what was already planned before the foundation of the world. It is an unbelievable thinking process to even dare to imagine the truth of these statements as to how big and great Jehovah is. David says:

Thou hast beset me behind and before, and laid thine hand upon me. Such knowledge is too wonderful for me; it is high, I cannot attain unto it. Whither shall I go from thy spirit? Or whither shall I flee from thy presence? **Psalm 139:5-6-7**

Oh that men would revere God for who He is and what great deeds He plans to draw out of us. Sometimes it is easy to think how great we are and what abilities we have and how self-capable we are in our great ignorance. Truly the discovery of the omnipotent God and His plans for you makes you learn to seek His counsel, guidance, and help in all things. It may be possible to amass great achievements, but none of which are what God planned for your life and therefore without reward. I pray this shall not be your portion.

It is therefore important to die to your ways and become alive to His. Renew your mind so as not to be conformed to the systems of this world, but to His will and glory. May we desire to see through His eyes and hear through His ears. Once again as the Apostle Paul said, "In Him we live and move and have our being." That is the only way to achieve the extraordinary heights set apart for every one singular person created on this earth to rejoice in; *the power of one.*

The power of one consumed by the Holy Spirit, informed by the Word of God and transformed to be a God-kind of achiever is a sight to behold. The world has been waiting for you. The power of one person in the hand of the stronghold-breaking and solution-giving God is and will be an outstanding success story to all generations.

You are a golden vessel in the hands of an outstanding Creator who designed you for commanding heights in your sphere of influence. You were made not just to follow success stories but to be followed as you walk in the high places according to the will of God. Success is not achieving great things, but doing the will of God with great contentment.

The Lord bless and keep you and let His countenance shine upon you throughout all the amazing days of your life. Enjoy your journey in destiny and leadership. Make the difference you were created for. May your mandate on this earth burn like God's eternal flames of fire without fail. May you enjoy your service to humanity with humility which is a key to greatness. I pray this day that your response to God's call will make you relevant in the eyes of all that see you and in the hearts of all that need you. Serve with a heart of excellence. May your time be protected as you lead with the power of conviction for a singular purpose on this earth. May the power of heaven drive you gloriously as a trusted individual in the plans of God. May you be celebrated as you cut through the chase of life, in the power of one to make a difference.